THE BATTLE FOR SURVIVAL AMONG INDIA'S TRIBES

DR. MUKTA GOYAL MR. KRITTIBAS DUTTA

Contents

Preface

India's Adivasi or tribal population is well-known for being a backward society. The scheduled tribes were the first people to settle in India and are the least advanced economically and socially. The Indian Constitution does not define Scheduled Castes or Scheduled Tribes. The constitution makes specific reference to Indian tribes in Articles 341 and 342. Indian tribes have residues in socioeconomically poor conditions. For the tribes, this situation has been restored to normal due in large part to the efforts of our governments. We are aware that India is a large nation with a large population, where many different ethnic groups have lived for a very long time. The defining characteristic of Indian culture and civilization today is unity in diversity. The authors of our constitution were aware that some racial or social classes had been deprived of a variety of privileges in our nation. The constitutional magistrate has argued that the constitution needs to include stronger protections for tribal people. In this way, our constitution has many special provisions to promote the scheduled Tribes in India.

Scheduled tribes are the most vulnerable segment of the Indian population from an economic, social, educational, and ecological perspective. The Government of India's most difficult undertaking since independence was the correct delivery of social justice to the scheduled tribes by improving their socioeconomic conditions delivery of social justice to the scheduled tribes by improving their living standards. In several five-year planning periods, our administrations have attempted to promote tribal development using a variety of models, methods, and theories. On the other hand, various government agencies across the nation have put in place several programs to develop the socioeconomic status of the Scheduled Tribes. The term "development" refers to the general rise in the standard of living. Development in tribal areas has, however, remained difficult since the beginning of time. The lives of the tribal people have undergone numerous changes recently, and both government and non-governmental initiatives have contributed to these changes. The empowerment of people, the equitable distribution of wealth and income, or the more general context of social natural resources are all ways that socioeconomic development might advance. Therefore, only with the involvement of tribes in project creation and implementation through working through their traditional system is their development conceivable.

The support of our parents and other family members, whose never-ending motivation helped us finish this book on schedule, made this effort possible. The amazing initiative of Notion press was the reason why the book as a whole took on its final form. We would like to thank every department of the publishing business.

Dr. Mukta Goyal
Krittibas Datta

CHAPTER ONE

PRE-INDEPENDENCE PERIOD AND UPRISING IN TRIBAL INDIA

Introduction

India is renowned for the adivasi or tribal people who live there. The term "adivasi" denotes that they were the lands earliest or original occupants and that they were native to the soil and their natural habitat. Tribes are typically thought of as simple social groups whose members cooperate for a common goal, such as welfare, and speak a same dialect. Tribes have a set habitat and territory, and their social organisation is built mostly on family links, cultural homogeneity, a shared conception of the gods and ancestors, as well as a shared dialect and folklore. In addition to giving them a sense of independence, self-identity, and respect, their environment and culture also give them the ability to stand together against any form of exploitation, oppression, or harassment by outsiders like zamindars, monarchs, British, and others.

The Tribes have developed a complex custodial way of life over the years. Tribes are a part of their territories, which are what make them who they are. In the past, the Tribes effectively functioned as independent "first nations." They were considered to be a part of the "unknown frontier" during the pre-colonial era, where the rule of the king actually did not reach. Tribes made their own rules independent of the particular king. The interaction between mainstream communities and indigenous tribes was altered by the arrival of Europeans and the following colonisation. Since ancient times, tribes in India have been shielded from the effects of attacks by foreign invaders, encroachments, wars, and other issues that affect mainstream civilization. Due to their remoteness, they lag behind their neighbouring communities in terms of socialisation, culture, and education. Since they were not seen as a danger to their kingdoms, local monarchs frequently had minimal interactions with them. Even though the rulers were aware of the terrible situations the tribes were in, they were in a bad position to act. Until the arrival of the British, this non-interventionist policy was maintained without interruption. The British established a straightforward system of managing the tribal areas under their colonial reign. When the British arrived, they brought with them many changes to their way of life as well as strangers into their domain. As a result, they were demoted from being landowners to being slaves and debts. Essentially, the uprisings were a defence of their independence and a reaction to this unwanted encroachment.

Analysis and Discussion

Due to the tribal people's generally inaccessible environments, such as distant hills, marshy or malaria-infested jungles, and hostile areas, contact between British officials and the tribal people remained challenging during the period of British control. The British relied on information from Christian missionaries and had a "leave them alone" approach. Instead of concentrating their authority on smaller tribal groups, they aimed to control the majority of the Indian population that was easily accessible. As a result, they continued to keep the indigenous people apart from the rest of the nation. They made little effort to free them from the influence of missionaries, the grasp of moneylenders, landowners, and contractors.

For the advantage of the class of people who were ardent supporters of British dominance in India, Lord Cornwallis established a system of land tenure in India in 1793. The government demanded rent payments from zamindars under the new land tenure system, which recognised them as landowners. As a result, zamindars could use land as both private property and a marketable good. With this method, the land was divided into small parts and given to several feudal lords. The tribals were quite upset about this new land tenure structure. These factors contributed to the unrest:

- The indigenous people's traditional economy was put in jeopardy, and they lost their claim to agricultural areas. The British government passed the first tenant law in 1859 to try and solve the issue, but it had no effect on helping tribal people and poor peasants.

- To keep tribes from fighting with established farmers, retired army personnel were permitted to settle on the outskirts of some tribal districts. As a result, tribal people developed a gulf of mistrust and suspicion toward the nearby non-tribals as a result of colonial policy.
- Forests, which are essential for obtaining sustainable means of subsistence, were now protected. The majority of tribal communities collect fuel, fodder, medicinal plants, roots, tubers, vegetable leaves, and other items from forests in order to survive. An important supply of protein is obtained through wild game hunting.
- The conservation of natural forests led to restrictions on shifting farming. Without giving the tribes alternative means of subsistence, this restricted their tribal rights to the forests. The British government created the First Forest Policy of 1894, a policy on forest reservation, to limit environmental exploitation. In many ways, it changed the tribal way of life. Formerly controlled by tribal groups, the forests gradually came under the administration of the Forest Department. Their historical right to the forest was no longer acknowledged, and they were no longer free to travel around the forest as they pleased. Tribes were forced out of their natural home, which led to them turning to criminal activity. Such tribes were subsequently classified as criminal tribes by the British authority.
- Incentives for native art and crafts were also withheld, which gave the tribes the impression that their goods fell short of expectations.
- Numerous tribe members were hired at minimum salary by mining and steel firms as a result of modernization. They had to take out loans to make ends meet. As payment for their obligations, the moneylenders instituted forced and bonded labour.

Important Tribal Uprising in 18th and 19th Century

The following are a few of the most significant tribal uprisings from the 18th and 19th centuries:

- **Rangpur, Bengal, Peasant Uprising (1783 AD)**

- The British began utilising revenue contracts to extort as much money as they could from peasants after capturing control of Bengal in 1757 AD.
- The peasants turned to the courts after the executives did little to address their complaints.

- Under the direction of Dirjinarain, they attacked the agricultural storage facilities and cutcheries owned by contractors or public authorities.
- Muslims and Hindus fought side by side throughout the uprising. The company's military staff eventually took charge of the situation and put a stop to the uprising.

- **Kol Rebellion in 1832**

- Among the tribes that inhabited Chhotanagpur and its environs were the Kols.
- Under their local leaders, they had full control, but when the British came, everything changed.
- Along with the British, traders and moneylenders arrived.
- The Kol family was consequently compelled to sell their property to foreign farmers and to face a hefty tax burden. As a result, many people ended up working as bonded labour.
- The British legal practises also infuriated the Kols.
- The Kols organised an uprising against the British and moneylenders from 1831 to 1832.
- They burned down houses while murdering several strangers. This bloody conflict continued for two years before the British utilised superior armaments to ruthlessly suppress it.
- It took troops from Benares and Calcutta to quell the Kol Revolt because it was so ferocious.

- **The Munda Ulgulan**

- The Mundas lived at Chotanagar.
- The Khunt Katti structure, a system of land sharing, was employed by the Mundas. After the British arrived, the Zamindari system took the place of the Khunkatti organisation. The tribal members were forced to labour, which resulted to debt.
- In the late 18th and early 19th centuries, there were a number of revolts against the British.
- An uprising was declared in 1894 by the charismatic and successful commander Birsa Munda.
- He has a public rebellion against the government planned. He encouraged others to skip paying their debts and taxes.

- Before his parole in 1897, he was apprehended and sentenced to two years in prison.
- In December 1899, he launched an armed uprising against the government and landowners.
- The Mundas burned down churches, mansions of landowners, government buildings, and other property owned by the British.
- In 1900, Birsa Munda had been captured. He passed away from cholera in prison at the age of barely 25.

Tribal Panchasheel and Indian policy at independence

The Constitution includes provisions for the socioeconomic advancement and self-determination of Scheduled Tribes in a number of its Articles. However, there hasn't been any national policy to assist make the constitutional requirements a reality. The management of tribal affairs has been governed by the Nehruvian Panchasheel, a set of five tenets outlined in 1952.

Jawaharlal Nehru thought that the development of the tribal people needed to happen through a gradual modernisation process, even while their culture needed to be preserved. For the tribal policy to be followed, he had developed the following five principles. As follows:

1. It is best to let tribes flourish at their own unique pace.
2. The land and forest rights of tribes should be honoured.
3. Without over-involving outsiders, tribal teams should be trained to handle administration and development.
4. It is important to pursue tribal development without upsetting tribal social and cultural structures.
5. The standard of their lives, not the amount of money invested, should be used to measure tribal development.

In order to hasten tribal development, the Indian government established a Ministry of Tribal Affairs for the first time in October 1999 after realising that the Nehruvian Panchasheel was long on generalities and short on specifics.

The Draft National Policy on Tribes has recently been released by the Ministry of Tribal Affairs. The Ministry will finalise the policy in light of input from tribal leaders, the concerned States, people, businesses in the public and private sectors, and NGOs. The National Policy is aware of:

1. The majority of Scheduled Tribes still experience poverty.
2. Their rates of literacy are low.
3. They experience sickness and undernourishment.
4. They are susceptible to being uprooted.

Additionally, it recognises that Scheduled Tribes as a whole serve as a repository for some indigenous knowledge and wisdom.

Recommendations and Findings

- The main reasons for each of these tribal uprisings in the 18th and 19th centuries were the quick changes made by the British to the economy, the government, and the land income structure. These changes upended the agrarian community, causing extreme and protracted suffering among its citizens.
- Tribal populations were horribly exploited after the British introduced moneylenders to them. The indigenous people were forced to work as labourers as a result of the newly established economic framework.
- The concept of exclusive ownership has replaced the common land ownership system that formerly existed in tribal societies.
- Utilization restrictions applied to hunting methods, shifting agriculture, and the use of forest products. The tribal people consequently lost their means of subsistence.
- In contrast to orthodox culture, which was characterised by class and status disparities, tribal life was often egalitarian. Tribals were demoted to the lowest levels of society when immigrants arrived.
- The very act of establishing law and order in remote locations exposed the tribes to pressure from more developed communities, even though British officials had no intention of interfering with tribesmen's rights and traditional way of life.
- Trading and moneylenders could now establish themselves under the protection of the British administration in the areas that had previously been essentially unadministered and unsafe for outsiders who did not enjoy the confidence and goodwill of the tribal inhabitants.

Conclusion

Since the arrival of the British till the present, administration in tribal areas has seen significant changes in the life of tribes, from total isolation to acculturation, assimilation, and incorporation into society. Contractors, bankers, businessmen, and other outsiders took advantage of tribes as a result of the colonial policy of "leave them alone." As a result, there was restlessness among the indigenous people, which gave rise to various movements. As a result, the tribal administration underwent a great deal of change, and new laws were created for the tribes' protection and advancement. With a few minor alterations, India continued to operate administratively in the same manner as the colonial powers after independence. Later on, however, tribal unity was viewed as the best course of action for the overall growth of the tribes.

CHAPTER TWO

INDIA'S TRIBAL POPULATION

Introduction

People who prefer to live alone in a closed society and who have common origins and culture are said to belong to a tribe. Indian tribes are the indigenous or native people who live all throughout the nation.

The Indian population is largely made up of tribes, and tribal culture is a vital component of our intangible national heritage. As a result, we need to be aware of some of India's most significant tribes.

On the Indian subcontinent's mainland, there are pockets of tribal people in almost every state and union territory. Mizoram (94.4 percent of the population), Lakshadweep (94 percent), Meghalaya (86.1 percent), and Nagaland are the locations with the highest percentage of tribal settlements (86.5 percent). There are significant tribal settlements in Madhya Pradesh, Orissa, Maharashtra, Rajasthan, Chhattisgarh, Assam, and West Bengal as well. In a larger sense, 8.6% of India's population belongs to the scheduled tribes.

The Indian Tribes

The Gonds, Bhils (or Bheels), Katkari, Tharu, and The Great Andamanese Tribes are the most well-known tribes in India.

According to the 2011 census, the Bhil tribal group is the largest tribe in India out of all of these tribes. It makes up an astounding 38% of all scheduled indigenous people in the nation.

Although the Bhils have a language named after them, the majority of them also speak Marathi, Gujarati, and the language of the state in which they are headquartered. The tribe is the largest in India and has origins in Maharashtra, Chhattisgarh, portions of Gujarat, Rajasthan, and even some of Tripura.

In addition, Bhil is one of the relatively few scheduled tribes in India known for its distinctive kind of art, known as Bhil Art. These works of art are meant to depict the tribe members' daily lives. They use natural colour pigments generated from various leaves and flowers along with Neem tree twigs and branches as brushes to create a variety of objects.

The deities and ancestors are portrayed in Bhil art in the form of dots painted over the background of the artwork in various colours and patterns, giving it a distinctive appearance.

The Gonds of Andhra Pradesh

India's largest tribal community, the Gond, has a population of around 12 million. The Gond speak a subset of the Dravidian language family found in South Central called the Gondi-Manda. Incompatible theories on their genesis are entertained by linguists, ethnographers, and anthropologists. Due to the inadequate resolution of the genetic data or the small number of samples, genetic investigations of these individuals have thus far suffered. We have therefore used high-resolution data to examine four geographically distinct Gond groups in order to acquire a more complete understanding of the ancient origins and genetic connections of the Gond with the neighbouring populations speaking Indo-European, Dravidian, and Austroasiatic languages. With some separation and differentiation, all Gond groups have a common ancestor. Instead of the other Dravidian tribes to which they are most closely connected linguistically, our allele frequency and haplotype-based analyses show that the Gond share major genetic heritage with the Indian Austroasiatic (i.e. Munda) communities.

The four main language groups and some isolated languages that make up India's linguistic landscape are mostly related to non-overlapping geographic divisions. Indo-European languages, which span a wide geographic area, including northern and western India, are spoken by the majority of the population. With a few exceptions, such as Brahui in Pakistan, Kurukh-Malto in eastern India, and Gondi-Manda languages in central India, Dravidian languages are mostly spoken in southern India. While Tibeto-Burman speakers can be found along the Himalayan edge and in the northeast of the subcontinent, Austroasiatic language speakers are dispersed in pockets, mostly in the eastern and central regions.

In contrast to the caste populations in India, only few tribes exist, with total populations in the millions. The Gond tribe is the most populous and has the most clearly defined clan system of all the central Indian tribes. They number around 12 million people and are primarily situated in eastern central India. There is no exact date for when Gond first appeared on the subcontinent. However, four of their kingdoms are dated to between 1300 and 1600 AD, and they are mentioned in the epic Ramayana. By the Middle Ages, these kingdoms had absorbed so much of the neighbouring Hindu culture's religious and cultural elements that the Gond cultures had developed into a socially more hierarchically structured tribal community. Gondi, Konda, Kui, Kuvi, Pengo, and Manda are all South Central Dravidian languages that are spoken by various segments of the larger Gond community. The Telugu language, which is mostly spoken in the state of Andhra Pradesh, including Telangana, is the most recent ancestor shared by the Gondi-Manda subgroup in terms of language. According to Robert von Heine-ethnographic Geldern's research, the local ancestral component of the Munda populations and a subset of Dravidian inhabitants represented by the numerous Gond language communities jointly constitute an older layer of the Indian subcontinent's population. Grigson adopted this hypothesis and argued that the Gonds were once a "pre-Dravidian" or "proto-Australoid" population that had undergone significant Dravidian influence. Following his research on the Gond and their closely related Dravidian language communities, Christoph von Fürer-Haimendorf came to the conclusion that these people were the last of an earlier primordial population that had been linguistically absorbed.

There is no other tribe in India's tribal population that can compare to the Gonds in terms of size and historical significance. With a population of well over four million in the late 1970s, the Gonds occupy a sizable portion of the Deccan and play a significant role in the intricate ethnic structure of the region where Indo-Aryan and Dravidian communities coexist.

Concentrations of Gonds remained to live in their traditional way of life in the highlands of the ancient Hyderabad State (now Andhra Pradesh) until the middle of the 20th century: feudal lords continued to act as tribal leaders and hereditary bards retained a treasure of myths and epic tales. Christoph von Fürer-Haimendorf started studying this group of Gonds at that time and spent the better part of three years in their settlements. He saw their everyday activities and intricate ceremonial rituals, and he also recognised the threat that more developed Hindu groups posing as they invaded the Gonds' habitat and vied for their ancestral territory.

Life, Livelihood and Education among the Katkari tribes of Maharashtra

Being one of Maharashtra's most marginalised tribes and having access to few resources, the Katkaris are socially, educationally, and economically underdeveloped. The current study examines the socioeconomic characteristics of the Katkari tribe through an examination of their socioeconomic indicators, including literacy, labour force participation, way of life, occupational pattern, health, and migration. A pilot case study of the Katkari tribes of the 85-hut Godpapad Adivasi Wadi in Maharashtra was carried out to investigate their living situations, means of subsistence, and reasons for having low levels of education. Direct observation and unstructured interviews were utilised as research methodologies to learn more about Katkari people and kids. The investigation indicated poor living circumstances, unstable livelihoods, and minimal education provision in the hamlet, however education was interrupted due to parents' seasonal travel in search of job. India's original inhabitants are the tribal people, who primarily live in the forested areas encircled by hills. They have a distinctive identity that is reflected in their own social structure, culture, language, and territorial affinity. According to its distribution, the tribal zone in India is typically divided into three zones: the north-eastern zone, the central zone, and the southern zone. The Himalayan region, as well as the hill and mountain ranges of North-Eastern India, make up the north-eastern zone. The area to the south of the Krishna River in Peninsular India makes up the southern zone. The central zone is located in the middle of Peninsular India's ancient hills and plateaus that separate it from the Indo Gangetic Plains (Planning Commission, India, 2007). The Katkari tribal community is recognised as the lowest in the social hierarchy by other Scheduled Tribes in the area and is classified as a particularly vulnerable, primitive, and tribal tribe in Maharashtra. Under the Constitution (Scheduled Tribes) order, 1950, the "Katkari" were first acknowledged as a Scheduled Tribe. In Maharashtra, the districts of Raigad, Thane, Pune, Nashik, and Ratnagiri are home to the majority of the Katkaris. (Tomar, 2004). The Katkari tribe is one of Maharashtra's most marginalised, underprivileged, and impoverished. They have restricted access to resources, which contributes to their social, educational, and economic backwardness. In the current study, the researcher conducted a pilot case study to examine the socio-economic indicators of the 85-hut Katkari Adivasi Wadi in Maharashtra, including livelihood, health, occupational pattern, migration, and education. Direct observation and unstructured interviews were utilised as study approaches to learn more about the adults and kids residing in the

Godpapad Adivasi Wadi.

Living Conditions in Katkaris

In the Sudhagad Taluka of the Raigad district, around 85 kilometres from Mumbai, Maharashtra, lies the tribal hamlet of Ghorpapad Adiwasi Wadi, which consists of a total of 85 huts or households. At the foothills of the Sahyadri Mountains in Godpapad Adiwasi Wadi, the researcher went to the homes of the Katkari people (Western Ghats). Their huts range in size from 100 to 150 square feet and have thatched roofs and unbaked brick walls that are often kachha or semi-pukka. Cow dung is used to clean the houses' walls and floors. The Katkaris prepare and consume meals using steel utensils and leaf-covered plates, respectively. The furnishings within the house are quite simple and comprise of a few kitchen utensils, a few items of clothing hung from a rope, and equipment for hunting and fishing. The study discovered that the locals use open defecation and lack basic sanitary facilities. They rely on a well for their drinking water, but in times of scarcity, they also use water from open ditches for various household needs, particularly during the monsoon season. Because of the sanitary problems this causes, illnesses including diarrhoea, dysentery, malnutrition, malaria, ringworm, intestinal infections, fever, etc. frequently result. When the researcher questioned some of the tribal members about how they treated illnesses, the Katkari tribal members responded that they only relied on traditional treatments that involved the use of herbal plants, tree roots, and bark, among other things, as well as the traditional knowledge passed down through the generations.

Occupations in Katkaris

Due to their predominately landless status, the Katkaris' traditional means of subsistence include hunting with crude tools and gathering insignificant forest products. They were compelled to relocate to the foothills of the forests, depriving them of their principal source of livelihood, as a result of government measures to stop deforestation and combat resource depletion. After speaking with a few Katkari males, the researcher learned that they are currently primarily engaged in two separate jobs, not simultaneously but rather in a cyclic fashion. They claimed to be agricultural labourers for other landed tribal ethnic groups in the neighbourhood from June to November, with the male members working as farm servants (known as gadi in the local language) and the womenfolk as daily paid labourers. These fields are primarily used for the production of rice, with ragi, udid (pulses), and khurasni (a regional kind of oilseed) serving as auxiliary crops. However, they claimed that because agriculture in these farmlands is dependent on rainfall and there are no options for irrigation, there is no room for double-cropping and as a result, these Katkari tribal people are left jobless at the conclusion of each agricultural season. To ensure their financial and food security, the Katkari men travel to other areas between December and May in search of work (mainly to other parts of Maharashtra, Andhra Pradesh, and Karnataka). They work in brick kilns. In order to support themselves and their families, the majority of Katkari males (about 98 percent) from Godpapad Adiwasi hamlet migrate to different regions of the nation during this periodic movement.

The Katkari are one of the only tribal communities in India that consumes rodents like the Indian bandicoot, black rat, and little Indian field mouse. They think that consuming rodent meat gives them strength and a long life.

Even though it was shown that 69.5 percent of Katkari youngsters had had any vaccinations, there was a substantial dropout rate for each shot.

The Eco-friendly Tharu Tribe

The Tharu culture is particularly environmentally conscious; all of this tribe's customs and practises have a strong connection to the natural world. They depend on nature for their homes, food, clothing, clothes, art, religion, economy, and many other aspects of life in order to maintain ecological equilibrium. The Earth, known to the Tharu as "Bhumsen" in their native tongue, is the principal deity they worship. In this society, the family structure is strong. Women enjoy high standing and sufficient social and economic rights in their family system. Although there is a patriarchal family system in this town, women have higher status and more rights, which is a measurable truth. Youth in Tharu prefer to change, thus they are competing for advancement. The process of cultural exchange is ongoing in the Tharu area because there are several other groups there thanks to industrialization and business. Tharu adolescents are drawn to a novel and alluring way of life. The old Tharu culture is under peril because they are ignoring their original tribal customs. They must receive modern education, communication, and technological advancements, etc. To maintain their identity, however, traditional culture must also be preserved.

The great Andamanese

The Andamanese, at least those who live on the southern island, don't build any form of dwelling. They enjoy sandy beaches with towering cliffs that provide wind protection. I frequently stumble across one of their makeshift homes when strolling down the beach close to Port Mouat; it consists of a hole dug out in the sand beneath an overhanging rock that can fit a single person. They rarely spend consecutive nights in the same sleeping arrangements. The people of the tiny Andaman build gigantic cottages that resemble beehives, with roofs that are almost at ground level. Their creation of strange objects like moving fish spears and arrows shows great innovation and the use of strong thinking to match means to ends. The arrow head, which is manufactured from iron taken from ships that have sunk nearby, is a triangular piece of flattened iron that is attached to the end of a short stick that is about four inches long. One to three iron barbs are also attached to the stick at the base of the head. This short stick's tip fits into a socket that is made for it at the very end of the arrow's shaft. A flattened thong (made of wood fibres) about eight inches long, linked at one end to the distal end of the shaft and at the other to the stick holding the head, also serves to preserve the connection between the head and shaft. They most likely learned how to build them through watching the Nicobarese huts on the nearby island of Car-Nicobar during some of their expeditions or by receiving instruction from their Nicobarese prisoners.

CHAPTER THREE

THE IMPACT AND FUTURE OF GOVERNMENT POLICIES ON THE INDIAN TRIBAL COMMUNITY

Introduction:

A democratic country needs to ensure that all the sections of the society get equal opportunity for growth & development. An equitable distribution of resources & equality before law are the hallmarks of our constitution. The development, in India, so far has been a bit lopsided as far as tribal population is concerned. There is a need to assimilate the Tribal community in the mainstream society in order to provide them opportunities for education, socio economic development and other welfare majors, while preserving there rich & unique cultural heritage. This paper examines the problems affecting the tribals, various government policies & schemes formulated for their upliftment and pit falls there in.

India has one of the largest Tribal populations in the world. But unfortunately, even after 75 years of independence , they are still socially & economically very week. There has been a wide spread exploitation of the tribal people in the name of development. They have been ousted from their natural habitat - forest. Although the government, both central & state, have formulated a number of policies & schemes for their development but still there is a lot left to be done. In the Pre Independence era , the Bretisheres adopted policies which were suitable to a colonial rule and served their best interest. Some of the laws fostered isolation of tribal communities from the main society while others had a more integral approach. After independence the government formed many policies & programs for the development of the tribals.

Constitutional Provisions of Scheduled Tribes in India:

In India, Tribal population is around 8.2 % of the total population living in the country. Most of the tribal population live in the states of Madhya Pradesh, Jharkhand, Chhattisgarh, Karnataka, Maharashtra, Rajasthan, Odisha, Gujarat, Andhra Pradesh and West Bengal. Madhya Pradesh has the highest number of tribal population with 14.7 per cent of the total tribal population in India. Maharashtra and Odisha stand in second and third position in the total tribal population. Uttar Pradesh has a least number of scheduled tribes with 0.56 percent of its total population ,than Tamil nadu and Bihar with 1.1 and 1.28 per cent respectively. The ministry of tribal affairs states that there are 705 tribal groups notified by the government of India. Odisha is a state where there is maximum number of tribal communities with 62 than any other state of the country.

Our constitution framers were aware of the fact that the tribal community in India need special provision in the constitution to establish social and economic justice. Keeping this in view many special provision were made in the Indian constitution for overall development.

The President of India has the constitutional power to declare tribal groups to be scheduled in relation to any state or union territory under Article 342. The term Scheduled Tribes first appeared in the constitution of India and define Scheduled Tribes under Article 366 (25) as "such tribes or tribal communities or parts of or groups within such tribes or tribal communities as are deemed under Article 342 to be Scheduled Tribes for the purposes of this constitution". Article 244 and 244a provide for Fifth and Sixth Schedule respectively for the special administration of the tribals. The Panchayats (Extension to the Scheduled Areas) Act, 1996 (PESA) in the Fifth Schedule Areas was introduced to secure local self-governance by the tribal people. The constitution provides for no prohibition of discrimination on grounds of religion, race, caste, sex or place of birth under Article 15, Equality of opportunity in matters of public employment under Article 16, Protection of certain rights regarding freedom of speech, under Article 19, Promotion of Educational and Economic interests of Scheduled Castes, Scheduled Tribes and other weaker sections under Article 46, Claims of Scheduled Castes and Scheduled Tribes to services and posts under Article 335.

Besides that, Article 330 and 332 provides for Reservation of seats for Scheduled Castes and Scheduled Tribes in the House of the People and in the Legislative Assemblies of the States respectively. Reservation in the seats of local self-government (Panchayat) is also provided under Article 243 D.

Government Policies and Programmes for Tribal Development :

The Government of India through various programmes and schemes has been improving the social, economic and political status of the tribal population.

Post-Matric Scholarship Scheme : Education is one of the vital fields that would greatly influence the lives of the tribes. This scheme delivers financial aid to the Scheduled Tribes students who are studying at the post-secondary level so as to enable them to complete their higher education. The ST students whose parent's annual income is 1.08 lakh or less stands to be eligible for the same.

Establishment of Ashram School in Tribal Sub-Plan Areas : The scheme provides for the establishment of Ashram schools in Tribal areas, ashram schools refer to such educational canters which not only cater to educational facilities but at the same time provide for accommodation for the children. This creates an environment conducive to learning and lays off the economic burden from their shoulders.

Rajiv Gandhi National Fellowship (2005-2006) : This is a central fellowship scheme that provides fellowship to Scheduled Tribes students for pursuing higher studies. Under this scheme, the ST student would get admission for full-time Ph.D. courses in academic institutions.

National Overseas Scholarships for Scheduled Tribes : This is a central financial assistance scheme for meritorious students who want to pursue higher education like- Master's degrees, Ph.D. and Post-Doctoral research programmes in foreign universities for certain disciplines of Engineering, Technology and Sciences. Through this, the government aims to increase the ambit of employment opportunities for the tribal people.

Vocational Training Canters in Tribal areas : This scheme provides opportunities for the scheduled tribes to develop themselves for a variety of job and self-employment in order to enhance their economic pursuits. This scheme is implemented through NGOs and State institutions where tribal trainees are appointed and are taught trade activities, research tasks, seminars and workshops for 6 months.

Coaching for Scheduled Tribes students: This scheme provides for coaching to the STs for competitive examinations . Tribal students gets coaching for all India Civil Services, State level Civil Services, and other competitive exams.

Adivasi Shiksha Yojana : This scheme is for those tribal students who want to pursue professional and technical education. This scheme provides for soft loans up to Rs. 10 Lakh with no interest.

Educational upliftment schemes : The government has launched schemes relating to hostels for ST girls and boys. These schemes stand to be most important as they provide accommodation to the students who are otherwise underprivileged because of the inaccessible location of villages. Also, in order to decrease the drop-outs rates of the ST a 'book bank' scheme was executed under which funds are provided for the buying of books.

Economic welfare schemes: The tribes need to be economically strong so that they can be socially and economically independent. The economic benefit schemes of the government aim to protect the tribals by forming special provisions under the Constitution of India and also caters to their economic needs by either giving long-term loans or giving grants with negligible interest rate. so, the following schemes would encourage the tribals to engage in new economic activities.

Term Loan Scheme : This scheme provides for Term Loans for viable business units costing up to Rs. 50 Lakhs whereas soft loans under this scheme are extended up to 90% of the unit cost. The loans are provided with a moratorium period and are to be repaid within 5 to 10 years according to the projected returns from the units.

Adivasi Mahila Sashaktikaran Yogna (AMSY) : It is an economic development scheme for the scheduled tribe's women. Under this scheme, a loan up to 90% for units for unit cost up to Rs. 2 Lakhs.

Micro Credit Schemes for Self-Help Groups (SHGs): This scheme caters to the small loan requirement for the tribal Self-Help Groups. Under Credit Schemes for Self-Help Groups, a maximum loan of fifty thousand is provided per member of the tribe, while a maximum of Rs. 5 Lakhs is provided for the SHGs. Further, the repayment period for this scheme is 5 years.

Special Central Assistance to Tribal Sub-Scheme : It is a 100% grant scheme from the Government of India as an effort for tribal development. The grant is utilized for the economic development of Integrated Tribal

Development Project (ITDP), Integrated Tribal Development Agency (ITDA), Modified Area Development Approach (MADA), Clusters, Particularly Vulnerable Tribal Groups (PVTGs) and dispersed tribal population.

Annual Grant Scheme Grants-in-Aid: This is an annual grant scheme from the government of India, under which according to the provisions of Article 275(1) of the Constitution of India, grants are released for 27 states for raising administration in tribal areas and for the welfare of tribal people. These grants are released to States timely with the aim to bridge the gap in few sectors such as- education, health and agriculture etc.

Development of Private Tribal Groups : Some Public cooperation schemes were initiated by Government. Primitive Tribal Groups refers to a group of a certain community under the Scheduled Tribes who have a declining population, low literacy rate and are economically backward. This scheme aims at planning the socio-economic development of the PTGs holistically so that they become the prime focus of action and in return, their quality of life could be improved. Activities under it include housing, land distribution, agricultural and cattle development, bringing nomadic PTGs to the settled mode of life.

Eklavya Model Residential School : The *Eklavya* Model Residential School is established to provide quality middle and high-level education and habitation to Scheduled Tribes students who live in remote areas. These residential schools help the students to undergo comprehensive development both mentally and socially. Such schools aid in their growth and empower them to be the torchbearers for their community. These setups help the families of scheduled tribes to send their children to study, learn and grow irrespective of them belonging to the most backward class in the country.

Development of forest village: There are tribal groups in the country who still continue to live in primitive conditions and are aggressive towards any change in their lifestyle. In India there are almost two thousand four hundred seventy four forest villages which make this scheme relevant. The activities under this programme are providing- primary education, healthcare, drinking water, sanitation, livelihood etc. so, development in this process would help the tribal groups to evolve and develop by living close in their home forest.

GovernmentProgrammes & Policies: Implications and Prospects

The Government of India through various programmes has been taking significant efforts for improving the social, economic and political status of the tribal population. Over the years the central government have made regular efforts in their holistic upliftment in the country ranging from launching schemes empowering the Scheduled tribes students to learn and grow, as per the necessities and requirement of the tribal people. The Government of India aiding families by granting long term loans.

The schemes launched seems to be only on formal papers but as their implementation and the expected results are far from achieving. But, even after long term efforts, the schemes of the government are not a sufficient for the development of tribal people. The benefits these schemes have merely reached to the rightful beneficiaries because of unawareness. In that case , NGOs, local media, local leaders, National and state governments, can work together jointly for creating awareness among the STs about their rights .

Conclusion:

In spite of all the efforts & policies mentioned earlier by the government the tribal community still isolated & backward.

The main reason for this lack of development is the tribal people are not adequately aware about the various policies & programmes made for them. The literacy rate among the tribals is very low. This lack of education makes them vulnerable to exploitation. Another aspect is the rich cultural heritage of the tribal society. They have age old customs & traditions which are unique to them and need to be preserved.

Thus, any policy for tribal development should not only focus on their social, economical growth but also sustain & maintain their culture & traditions.

Then & only then the identity of the tribal populous will be preserved & flourished.

CHAPTER FOUR

THE CUSTOMS AND METHODS OF INDIA'S INDIGENOUS PEOPLES' GROWTH

Introduction

The true identity of the ancient peoples is hidden in the word 'indigenous people'. Indigenous peoples are today identified with the so-called civilized society of Calculated.

If we go back to the thousands of years old Indian civilization from today, if we try to find the history of these indigenous peoples, then we will see that these indigenous communities are our true indigenous peoples of India.

The ancient Indian subcontinent is considered to be the riverine country of the world. By plundering and occupying the lands of this country as well as by seizing the lands of this country, the foreign armies have plundered the wealth of the people by force. That is why even today they are identified as a neglected, neglected, helpless, out-of-society barbaric tribe.

As the environment of the world has changed, so has the culture of India. Indigenous peoples have come up with new cultures based on mixed cultures in contact with different relatively advanced nations. But it is true that No. They moved away to a distant world, clinging to a different orthodox culture and becoming accustomed to living.

Indigenous culture:

Indigenous communities continue their traditional way of life by incorporating their traditional way of life. In fact, this society learns to live by blind superstition, religious sentiments, ancient traditions and surrendering to nature. In their social system, adults are highly respected. By placing them in the seat of the guru of the society, they are considered as the bearers and carriers of the society. They are the real controllers of the society. Most of these adults are uneducated and orthodox. As a result, the rules and regulations of the society bound by them and with them the conduct becomes unscientific and irrational. As a result, the life of the people became miserable due to falling into the trap of irrational rules and regulations.

In many cases the neo-youth communities became rebellious. Another aspect of tribal life is simplicity. They never examine the behavioral aspects of logic. They become blind believers and voluntarily accept everything without any hindrance without any hindrance. Who completely stopped the expansion of society Carrier? Indigenous Indian communities across India endure hard work and hardship. Their culture is to overcome the impenetrable and bring victory. Indigenous culture does not have the intention of accomplishing the task by means of comfort, ease and cunning. Naturally, just as one has to conquer every natural adversity, so one has to survive in the battle of life by overcoming the onslaught of the adversary. This is made possible by the fact that they are the bearers and carriers of the most hard working and unequal brave culture. Indigenous life means living without fear. Living without giving up. In the face of all kinds of adversity, saving lives, they have never had the plague of tidiness in their social culture, nor have they borrowed from Aishwarya Upotokan. As soon as the sun rises, from the old to the young children, they prepare for the physical labor. With great joy, they all invest their labor in the workplace together. Unlike other advanced civilized inhabitants of the world and India, they are not accustomed to the sophisticated way of life of modern information technology resources. The main step of this indigenous community is physical labor. Indigenous peoples are accustomed to a very simple and unpretentious way of life. They think that the well-being of the family is more important than the cost of living. Indigenous society is not in the culture. In tribal culture, the Guru is a great believer in tradition. That is why they prefer to run the family society by putting the oldest people of the family in the seat of guru, under his direction.

Indigenous peoples and cultures are very religious. In their culture, they are determined to adhere to the traditional customs or rules of purchase. So another aspect of the indigenous culture is that on a particular day or time of the year, they worship according to certain rules and rituals. The main step of the indigenous culture is to become a manual laborer. The saline saline soils of the sea produce crops by hard labor and meet the needs of the human race and build up the country's grain reserves. In the same way, one of the elements of culture is animal husbandry. That is why the indigenous people keep a lot of animals and birds. In their culture, the housekeepers and masters of the house go out of the house every day to earn money by working hard all day long. Another aspect of the indigenous culture is that the sons and daughters of the children of their families cooperate with the parents in every task from their childhood. In this way they become proficient in any task from a young age. Just like every human being who is well educated in childhood and grows up is guided in the path of true ideals. There is no place for indulgence in indigenous culture. So they cannot build up a wealth of riches by hard earned money for long life. They do not have the means to take initiation and become self-reliant in the indigenous culture and to make continuous efforts or encouragement. The whole country and the whole of India and the world will benefit if we can enlighten the indigenous culture in the light of good education by accepting the modern services of advanced social system in the light of modern education system. The light of higher education has not yet penetrated into the indigenous culture in such a way that it has not been possible to develop the indigenous culture towards modern education. Indigenous culture is a matter of learning like the Indus philosophy at the point Sitting. If the Indian culture is not fully integrated with the tribal culture and a culture of universal acceptance is not developed, the development of the tribal community will never be possible. Indigenous Himachal tribal culture exists across every state of India. Although their expansion and cultural development has been completed at a very slow pace, it is moving forward - admittedly.

The Chief Minister of the state himself is the head of the tribal society. As a result, she is the bearer and carrier of this society. So this proves that the development of Indian indigenous culture is happening. Indigenous culture in Madhya Pradesh today is fighting with the mainstream. Some separatist extremist groups are trying to keep the indigenous people living in economically underdeveloped states like Chhattisgarh in an atmosphere of illiteracy and superstition by giving wrong messages, pushing back their culture. But they are not able to hold on to this culture. In this way the indigenous culture has improved a lot today and has stood tall in the field of education. But their invisible evil hand has never been able to keep the indigenous culture in the grip of underdevelopment. In this way the indigenous culture has improved a lot today and has stood tall in the field of education. In the same way, the indigenous culture has improved a lot in the field of education today. Finding the comfort of their own life in their own culture.

This language has been recognized as one of the major languages in West Bengal. At present, this language has been used in many new schools. In the same way, the indigenous peoples of Nepali, Garo, Thesis, Naga, Jayantia etc. cultures are becoming able to live a better life today. Indigenous culture has undertaken a number of initiatives to advance the path of development, which, of course, deserves significant credit. At the same time, it must be acknowledged that this is a relentless, selfless effort to bring indigenous culture to a better place. The various developmental programs of some missionary schools, Bharatseva Ashram, Government Kendriya Nabodaya Vidyalaya, etc., all public service activities, as well as providing free high quality education free of cost with the provision of accompanying meals throughout India through their relentless activities across. Their successful endeavors have certainly led to the rise of indigenous culture as well as the overall expansion of indigenous society as well as socio-economic development. Boys and girls of indigenous culture living from the hills to the sea level are able to fill the gaps of the society by getting education through English. The development of social assessment has taken place.

As a result, thousands of indigenous boys and girls are coming forward to become self-reliant by learning modern English. In the same way Bharatseva Ashram, through their service-oriented services, has made it possible for the indigenous communities of Asimudra Himachal to improve their culture by providing various services as well as better education in their socio-economic fields. However, it goes without saying that the bearers of this simple, straightforward, unpretentious culture are still being misled by misunderstanding. As a result of which today they are being misled with wrong tag by organizing development and action sacrifices of the ruling classes of the country. Indigenous peoples need to be immersed in the main mantra of Indian culture by providing proper employment as well as proper education. Only then will the development of indigenous culture take place. Let us now take a clear look at the types of tribes. India is a vast country which has resulted in a huge number of tribes scattered all over the sub-continent in this vast country like the subcontinent. We need to get a clear idea about all these tribes. Then we will try to know more about the culture of each of them. There is no other country in the world with such a large number of tribes like India, let alone any other continent.

Santal culture is present all over West Bengal, Jharkhand and Bihar."However, throughout the West Bengal, the predominance of Santal tribes living in the country is much higher. The people of the Santal tribe do not worship any deity .Usually the people of this tribe worship male deities .Most of the age of the society is in the seat of respect by almost everyone .Most of the elders of the society take the responsibility of worship .They are called Majhi Baba in the local language .These sailors or priests are not one or single person .In this society, up to three or four people are engaged in worship .There is no specific book or calendar of tribal society .They themselves choose a particular time of the year and worship at their own convenience.The people of the Santal community believe in the religion of nature .That is why they worship when the harvest comes or the production of good crop comes .All the members of the same community living in the same village perform any ritual together .In this society, it is customary to sacrifice fruit or chicken and sometimes goat for a loan, even if it is a personal curse .The identified majhis of the society build a earthan high space altar for worship . The raised earthen space is well covered with soil to make it smooth and beautiful and eye-catching. If every family living in this society had a clean and tidy house on that particular puja day .Marangburu is the deity worshiped in Santal society. It is revered as an awakened deity with great reverence. The pujota of this tribal society starts from the time of swinging of Bengali Hindu society. Like the rebirth ceremonies of the Bengali Hindu society, their day-to-day life depends a lot on the will of the people living in that society . All the elderly people living in the tribal society sit together and decide the day of their scheduled puja on the basis of discussion. It is called Jaher puja in Santali language .Besides, they perform pujo etc. in Mamore at different times of the year .All these pujas are usually performed in the month of Baishakh Jyeshtha. In English, usually in the month of February-March .The demands of indigenous peoples are very limited and small .They pray to the god Marangburu for the well-being of their children and for the well-being of the family. In the language of the indigenous Santals, the ceremonies are called Baha and Sarai .The altar on which the priests of the tribal society, i.e. the father of the boatman, worship, is called Zahir Sthan .In addition, the Santal tribal community celebrates the Badhana festival in October every year .This vessel festival is celebrated for three days .This festival is mainly worshiped for the purpose of Cow which is called God worship .The festival are also called Cow Khutan festival .The guru is tied to a pole so that they do not get hurt and their god is not displeased with the king ,so they want to forgive to God .Be members of the Santal community vow to God to fulfill various desires .Indigenous peoples have been addicted to water and intoxicants since childhood and even offer samras to satisfy their deities .Indigenous people drink water and drugs called Hariya at any event .There is no caste distinction in the tribal community and all people have equal status and dignity in the society .Indigenous Santal community has no specific professional position in the society .In the indigenous Santal society, marriage is not a commodity .If boys want to marry girls, they have to pay a price to the father of the daughter .Usually between the two societies the fathers sit in the desert between the two villages and fix the wedding day .Usually there is a mediator to settle two marriages which is said to Raibar .When their wedding day is over, they have to be invited by Giratala .Gira is the first to invite those who belong to this indigenous Santal society, who are identified as bearers and carriers, i.e. Majhibaba.Gilatla is the number of seats given in the formula for how many days are left for a pure wedding day to come and each must be dipped in yellow water.There is another custom in this society which is to give cows .After the marriage, when the sun comes to the father-in-law's house, a young cow is provided by the daughter .The boy will either arrange to take her home or give her the responsibility of keeping someone in the vicinity of the girl's house .

Let's start with the northeastern states:

Arunachal Pradesh is inhabited by Abar, Apatani, Mishmi etc. Abar tribes live in Siyat, Subarnasiri and Dibong districts of Arunachal Pradesh. They can easily adapt to the difficult situation and become able to live a life. They are very physically hard. They are very flexible in living in unfavorable environment. They use the rain water and cut the steps of the hill and cultivate. This is the main livelihood of their society. Their local name is "Adi" tribe. Other tribes are usually Buddhists and Christians. They are only able to produce it in the rainy season. So they engage in a large-scale social event during the only harvest of the year. Which is called Solung festival in the local language. A type of tribe called "Apatini" lives at Zero Point in Subarnasiri district of Arunachal Pradesh. They work very hard. The people of this tribe are very environmentally conscious. Their main livelihood is cultivation. They make a living by cultivating in rain water. They also cultivate by cutting the steps at the foot of the mountain. They work hard physically. The people of this tribe are Christians and Buddhists. The people of this tribe celebrate two major festivals every year. Stays. Inevitably, both festivals are crop-centric. "Dr" for a good harvest the festival, "Miokko" is celebrated to rejoice after the harvest. A type of tribe called "Mishmi" lives in Dibat Lohit Anj district of Arunachal Pradesh. Life is a livelihood. The people of this valley trade with nearby Tibet.

This time we will move on to the states of Madhya Pradesh and Chhattisgarh:

These two states are inhabited by tribes like Baiga, Vil, Gand, etc. They usually live in the jungles. They want to separate their culture from the general civilized society we can recall that the largest number of tribes live in these two states in the whole of India.

Baiga Tribes:

These Baiga tribes live in Madhya Pradesh, Chhattisgarh, Uttar Pradesh, Jharkhand etc. Their occupation is to collect roots, honey, vegetables, wood, hunting animals, fishing, etc. They are nomadic in nature. They have their own style of worship in life culture.

Vil Tribes:

The Vil tribes live in the states of Madhya Pradesh, Rajasthan, Gujarat, etc. In other words, they make a living by donating daily labor on other people's land or at home. They have their own language. The people of this tribe love to have a lot of fun. They love to live a life of great pleasure.

Gold Tribe:

These Gond tribes live in the states of Maharashtra, Orissa, Madhya Pradesh, etc. The areas inhabited by these "Gond" tribes. They are called Gawwana Leo. These tribes have their own language. Their name is "Gondibhasha". The people of this tribe have their own religion, their own language. So they are strong in their culture. The people of this tribe worship snakes.

Cole Tribe:

They live in Madhya Pradesh, Chhattisgarh, Bihar, Assam, Meghalaya, Tripura and other states. They make their living by farming, hunting animals in the forest, collecting honey, collecting forest leaves, etc. They are guided by their own culture. Their society is male Tantric. Men set the policy for everything. The family and society are governed according to their principles. They have their own language. The name of this language is Baghlandi language. They speak this Baghalanti language. They live in small villages with small families. In their local language, the villages are called

"Kolhan".

Santal, Munda, Orao Tribes:

These Santals live in West Bengal, Bihar, Jharkhand, Assam, Nepal. Their main livelihood is farming, animal husbandry, animal hunting, day labor etc. The people of this tribe depend on their own culture. In their culture, dances, songs, weddings and rituals are celebrated in their own language. Harvest festival is celebrated in winter. The local name of the festival is "Sohraya Shatachara I will bury the tree in a certain season". Their only language is 'Santali' which is written or written in the form of 'Alchiki'.

Munda:

The Munda people are mainly from West Bengal, Bihar, Jharkhand and Assam. The people of this tribe make a living by cultivating livestock. They have their own language. Their language is Mundari language. In many cases they follow the same culture as the Santal tribe.

Orao Tribes:

Orao tribes live in the states of West Bengal, Bihar, Jharkhand, etc. They usually live in the vicinity of the forest. They make a living by climbing wood and honey from the forest. They also make a living by hunting animals. This tribe also has its own language .This language is used to communicate ideas in their society. The name of their language is Kuruk "language". This time we will look back at the tribal inhabitants of the Andaman and Nicobar Islands.

Jarwa Tribes:

The people of the Jarwa tribe usually live in the southern and central Andaman Islands. They are still accustomed to living like primitive uncivilized people in the deep and inaccessible environment of the forest at the foot of the mountain. Even today, they do not allow anyone to enter into the secrets of their own culture. Even today, in the 21st century, they do not use any costumes. They do not have a specific livelihood. Like the underdeveloped primitive people, their way of life is still like that of the uncertain animals. They hunt animals in the forest and sometimes burn raw meat and sometimes half-boiled to fill their stomachs. Besides, they are much more self-sufficient and internal in order to survive in the battle of life by fighting with animals. Moreover, the fruits of the forest, the main herbs, the roots of the soft tree and the juice they eat, they live far away from the common civilized society because they are very violent nature like animals. The entry of any other race or traveler into their primitive culture is extremely annoying. As the Great Andaman Trunk Road passes through the tribal habitat, it has become a source of considerable discomfort to them.

The Ongi tribe:

The Ongi people live mainly in the Little Andaman region. They are mainly of the Sasabar class. Their livelihood is hunting. They do not have a permanent place to live.

Sentinel tribes:

The Sentinel tribes live on the North Sentinel Island in the Andaman and Nicobar Islands, and are part of a civilized society. They do not live near them. They have a very violent mentality. They do not want to let the people of other races know about the people of civilized society, they do not want anyone to come near the edge of their area of residence. They think twice about trying to kill him if they try to approach him, leaving their culture largely unknown.

Toda Tribes:

The Toda tribes live in the state of Tamil Nadu, India. Their culture is to make a living by raising animals. They also make a living by farming. They build and live in houses with small bamboos and leaves. They have their own language, which is called Tora. They live in small villages. They tend to be very social. Bhara is a strong believer in God. They build their own temples with their own style and characteristics. Stays. They make life very enjoyable. So in order to diversify their daily life, they organize various social rituals and they perform those rituals in a splendid manner.

Garo Tribes:

The Garo tribes also live in Meghalaya, Assam, Tripura, Nagaland and Bengal. Because in the family culture of other provinces, fathers are usually the head of the family and society. But in the culture of the Garo tribe, family and society are completely matriarchal. That is, women become the head of the family and society. The whole family and society is run in the name of women. That is, the omnipotent Katu of the family and society is the oldest woman in a family. All the members of the family will be known by the title of this woman. Their main occupation is agriculture. However, fruits and vegetables are cultivated step by step in the hilly areas. Besides, fishing, doing business, day labor, etc., are their livelihood. They have their own language for exchanging ideas, which is called Garo language.

Khasi Tribes:

Khasi tribes usually live in Meghalaya and Assam. They survive in the rugged underdeveloped environment of the mountains, tolerating the unfavorable weather to sustain life. It goes without saying that no agricultural grain is produced in this environment. By grasping the tourism industry, they want to survive in the war of life. However, on a somewhat flat slope of the hill, a small area is cultivated, but it is of very low quality and produces less youth. As the Khasi tribes endured great hardships, they were able to cope with the adversity of life and survive. Both the family and the society of the Khasi tribes are matriarchal. The head of the family is an old woman and the family is run in her name. The surname of the woman determines the surname of all the members of the family. A significant feature of their culture is that no other nation has the right to enter this society in any way. In other words, if a rich person wants, he cannot buy land in their society and live in a house. The Khasi tribes are generally Christian. They celebrate the Nankrema festival in November every year after the harvest once a year.

Naga Tribes:

Naga tribes live in the states of Nagaland, Arunachal Pradesh, Assam, Manipur etc. Known as warrior tribes in the history of the Naga tribe, they are very violent in nature. They follow the patriarchal system in their society and family system. Although they are violent in nature, many are cultivating in the touch of modern civilization. In the present times, the Naga tribes have become more and more civilized, as a result of which they have become aware of the working methods of modern farming and are cultivating good crops and producing a lot of crops. The Naga tribes have their own advanced culture. As a result, they perform various cultural programs in their own way, following their own customs and art techniques. There are different groups among the Naga tribes. They speak their own language in their respective groups, such as "Angami", "Aao", etc. They are known by many names as Nagawada war favorite tribes, such as "Chat", "Jepam, Mao, Tangkhul, etc." The Naga people love to have a lot of fun. So they have their own style of dancing and singing. At certain festivals, they celebrate by wearing their own costumes and displaying their art techniques. Every year, the people of different Naga tribes celebrate the "Hargbill" festival together, between one and ten days in December each year.

Bhutia Tribes:

Apart from Uttarakhand, Himachal Pradesh, Sikkim, Jammu and Kashmir, Arunachal Pradesh and Ladak, Bhutia tribes live in Nepal. The Bhutia tribes are nomadic in nature. Moreover, they also make a living through animal husbandry. Their family and the culture of the social system is the patriarchal family. The elders of the family pay homage to it with great reverence, their family discipline and creativity are very strong. Dance, song, entertainment are prevalent in their culture. They have their own costumes. Bhutia Buddhists have their own musical instruments for their entertainment.

Steps tobe taken for the development of Indian tribal culture:

India is a multi-lingual, multi-cultural, multi-religious country. This glorious country is inhabited by many traditions. As a result, we have to make an effort to build a modern India by bringing all nations to the door of equal development and bringing them to the pinnacle of success. Those who are still considered as underdeveloped tribes have become detached from the modern culture by deviating from the original society and their own group or tribe is falling behind from the culture of the modern civilized world. It has to find the right reasons and identify the right aspects of each weakness. After all, every cause has to be solved by eliminating the problem. Therefore, in this great work, forgetting the party, opinion, race, religion and provinciality of government and non-government organizations, organizations, clubs, various voluntary organizations, etc., everyone should come forward with an open mind. All political parties must rise above petty interests and devote themselves to the service of the real tribes. Only then will the culture of the tribes develop. So is the country. The world will be able to reach the peak of development. At certain festivals, they celebrate by wearing their own costumes and displaying their art techniques.

Looking back at the tribes around the world:-

Indigenous peoples were first considered as the national hill tribes of that country.Many tribal group live all over the world. So, after a long discussion in the UN about their definition and rights, no decision was taken by all. In each case, they have seized it, despite obstacles we can scarcely imagine. "So they have their own culture in every country, every country has its own people today.

About 5,000 indigenous peoples live in more than forty countries on five continents .The number of those indigenous peoples scattered all over the world will be around 30 to 35 cores. Without proper policy determination, they are marginalized and integrated. When they have protested for their rights against the injustice of the country that is when the powerful ruling class of the country stopped any of their movements by unjust exploitation and even assassination. In 1982, the United Nations recognized the first indigenous peoples in the international arena .Indigenous people's right to self-determination is a relief to every state .However, Australia, Canada, New Zealand, India, China, Latin America and many other countries have the most tribes.

The ways to bring the tribes back to the mainstream of life are: -

1) All over India, the tribes have to make a draft which is complementary to the social, economic, quality of education only.

2) Adequate education, food, housing services should be ensured in well-developed tribal areas.

3) Money should be allocated in the annual budget of the central government for the tribes by making a definite outline. At the same time, the state government has to allocate a certain amount of money for tribal development in the same way according to its capacity.

4) For the nomadic tribes to build a permanent place in a specific place in the country, they must be confined to a specific place by allocating that specific place. Then it will be possible to keep them confined within certain areas.

5) In order to eradicate superstition and superstition, various seminars, fairs, discussion rounds, camp dances and song and entertainment should be arranged in the jewels of the tribe.

6) To earn the trust and confidence of the tribes,

7) The bearers of modern civilized society.

8) The tribes must be made aware and interested in the fact that they have equal rights to all the resources of the country.

9) It is necessary to awaken the feeling among the tribes that we have equal rights in this country, this soil, every element of this earth.

10) The people of the tribal community should be made aware of the modern civilized society of the world.

11) Continuous development, keeping close contact with them and modernizing them by mixing with them.

12) All the logistics senders are essential for social development.

13) More and more self-help organizations and resources need to come forward to bring these tribes back into the mainstream of life.

(14) It is essential to identify all the tribal areas and provide them with all the necessities of life as well as roads, schools, colleges, parks, auditoriums as recreational areas.

15) To encourage the mainstream of life by providing improved equipment, proper training, as well as training in other technical skills, handicraft training and supply of suitable equipment and raw materials in order to encourage the livelihood of the tribes.

16) The government must make arrangements for the tribes who are interested in animal husbandry, to provide them with young birds, food, medicine and other suitable training.

17) The Central Government of the country should make arrangements for the implementation of specific plans

18) So that every Indigenous family becomes self-reliant in the socio-economic field.

19) It is necessary to ensure the participation of the people of the tribal community in every conduct and function of the society.

20) In order to awaken devotion, devotion, devotion and devotion to the country, every tribe should be ensured to join multiple armed forces including army and forest forces. If necessary, inclusion in the tribe should be ensured by introducing conservation policy.

In this way, the whole of India will be in the best position in the world if the development and expansion of the cultures of the tribes scattered in different parts of India can be brought together and developed.

CHAPTER FIVE

TRIBES AND INDIAN CONSTITUTION

Introduction

India is a democratic nation that attempts for the socio-economic upliftment of all sections in the society as well as the conservation and protection of tribal culture and their way of life. According to Article 342 of the constitution, scheduled tribes are the tribal communities which have been declared after consultation with the Governor as such by the president by public notification. The constitution of India provides for uniform rule over the whole country but certain regions of the country are governed by special provisions to ensure the protection of cultural identities, customs and economic and political interests of the original inhabitants of these areas. These regions include the tribal hills of the North Eastern States. Assam, Arunachal Pradesh, Manipur, Nagaland, Mizoram, Meghalaya and Tripura, the state of Jammu and Kashmir and the regions known as the "Scheduled Areas" . The scheduled areas are those tribal inhabited areas which are located in other parts of the country than the North-East-India.

(1)Tribal Communities have developed in Independent India, with having a prominent figure like Dr. B.R. Ambedkar who fought for the rights of weaker sections of society. "He clearly identified socio economic backwardness of tribals. He knows that tribals are the people who lived with the freedom without much any influence from the outside society. They used to have autonomy and rights over the forest resources. But, they had lost all those privileges with the advent Britishers in to the forest areas with their draconian forest laws and land regulations. Tribals had haunting memory by experiencing political, economic and cultural hegemony from east India Company. Company's policy on tribals is to exploit their labour for generating revenue and controlling the forest resources by enacting new forest laws. They constructed modern transport systems likes railways and road ways in order to plunder the heavy raw materials (primarily agricultural products like cotton, jute, indigo, tobacco, rubber tea etc.) to their home lands. Since the Cost of building these modern transport was required more investment in capital and labour, so they did it by exploiting the tribals labour and forests for wood. In order to fulfill this huge investment, they started extracting more revenue, particularly from agricultural land. Forest lands also cleared for agriculture and tribals were forcefully brought under new laws, not permitted to mobile freely and not allowed to use forest resources, which was very essential part of their live."[1]

(ii)The framers of the Constitution took note of the fact that certain communities in India were suffering from extreme social, educational and economic backwardness. They needed special consideration for safeguarding their interests and for their socio-economic development. The term 'Scheduled Tribes' first appeared in the Constitution of India. Article 366 (25) of the Constitution of India defined scheduled tribes as "such tribes or tribal communities or parts of or groups within such tribes or tribal communities as are deemed under Article 342 to be Scheduled Tribes for the purposes of this constitution". The tribes are the autochthonous or native people of the land who are believed to be the earliest settlers in the Indian Peninsula. They are generally called *Adivasis* implying original inhabitants. the ancient and medieval literature mention a large number of tribes living in India.India has one of the largest and diverse tribal populations in the world.

Unlike the scheduled castes, there are differences among the scholars on the criteria to identify the tribals or the scheduled tribes. The tribals follow multiple religions in the country-Buddhism, Christianity, Islam or their indigenous religions. There is almost unanimity among the scholars on certain characteristics of the tribals.

These characteristics are as:

1) Their close association with nature, mainly the forests,

2) Relatively traditional means of cultivision and less development market,

3) Near absence of the rigid division with in the community and discrimination on the basis of birth, unlike the caste division among the Hindus,

4) Presence of the traditionalchiefs or headmen and better position of women as compared to the non-tribals,

5) Attachment/ reverence to traditional customs and culture. Article 342 of the Constitution attributes isolation, backwardness and cultural distinctiveness as the characteristics of the Scheduled Tribes."The President may, with respect to any State or Union territory, and where it is a state, after consultation with the Governor there of by public notification, specify the tribes or tribal communities or parts of or groups within tribes or tribal communities which shall, for the purposes of this constitution, is deemed to be scheduled tribes in relation to that state or Union Territory, as the case may be.Parliament may by law include in or exclude from the list of Scheduled tribes specified in a notification issued under clause(1) any tribe or tribal community or part of or group within any tribe or tribal community, but save as aforesaid, a notification issued under the said clause shall not be varied by any subsequent notification. Thus, the first specification of Scheduled Tribes in relation to a particular State/ Union Territory is by a notified order of the President, after consultation with the State governments concerned. These orders can be modified subsequently only through an Act of Parliament. The above Article also provides for listing of scheduled tribes State/Union Territory wise and not on an all India basis. The criterion followed for specification of a community, as scheduled tribes are indications of primitive traits, distinctive culture, geographical isolation, shyness of contact with the community at large, and backwardness. This criterion is not spelt out in the Constitution but has become well established. It subsumes the definitions contained in 1931Census, the reports of first Backward Classes Commission 1955, the Advisory Committee (Kalelkar), on Revision of SC/ST lists (Lokur Committee), 1965 and the Joint Committee of Parliament on the Scheduled Castes and Scheduled Tribes orders (Amendment) Bill 1967 (Chanda Committee), 1969.In exercise of the powers conferred by Clause (1) of Article 342 of the Constitution of India, the President, after Consultation with the State Governments concerned have promulgated so far 9 orders specifying the Scheduled Tribes in relation to the state and union territories. Out of these, eight are in operation at present in their original or amended form. One order namely the Constitution (Goa, Daman & Diu) Scheduled Tribes order 1968 has become defunct on account of reorganization of Goa, Daman & Diu in 1987. Under the Goa, Daman & Diu reorganization Act 1987 (18 of 1987) the list of Scheduled Tribes of Goa has been transferred

to part XIX of the Schedule to the Constitution (Scheduled Tribes) Order, 1950 and that of Daman & Diu II of the Schedule of the Constitution (Scheduled Tribes) (Union Territories) Order, 1951."[2]

(iii)Article 244 of the Constitution makes special provisions for the administration certain areas called 'scheduled Areas' in States other than Assam, Meghalaya, Tripura and Mizoram even though such areas are situated within a State or Union Territory, Presumably because of the backwardness of the people of these areas. Subject to legislation by parliament, the power to declare any area as a Scheduled area is given to the President and the President has made theScheduled Areas Order, 1950, in the pursuance of the power. These are areas inhabited by Tribes specified as Scheduled Tribes, in states other than Assam, Meghalaya or Tripura. Special provisions for the administration of such areas are given in the Fifth Schedule. The tribal areas in the states of Assam, Meghalaya, Tripura andMizoram are separately dealt with and provisions for their administration are to be found in the Sixth Schedule to the constitution. Part x of the constitution is concerned with the administration of scheduled Areas and Tribal Areas. The constitution makes special provisions for the administration of certain areas called scheduled areas presumably because of the backwardness of the people of these areas.

"The principal object of these specific provisions in the Fifth Schedule Fifth and Sixth Schedules is to protect the interests and rights of the tribals in their land, habitat and economy; and to preserve the communities customs and tradition and to ensure a faster socio-economic development in the "Scheduled Areas". The "Scheduled Areas" as defined in Part C of the Fifth Schedule are "such areas as the President may by order declare to be Scheduled Areas". The criteria for the declaration of any area as a Scheduled Area under the Fifth Schedule as recommended by the First Scheduled Areas and Scheduled Tribes Commission also known as Dhebar Commission are: a) Preponderance of tribal population, b) Compactness and reasonable size of the area, c) Under-developed nature of the area, and d) Marked disparity in the economic standard of the people. These Scheduled Areas are predominantly inhabited by tribes specified as "Scheduled Tribes" and located in the states of Andhra Pradesh, Telangana, Bihar, Chhattisgarh, Gujarat, Himachal Pradesh, Madhya Pradesh, Jharkhand, Maharashtra, Orissa and Rajasthan. Para 6(2) in Part C of the Fifth Schedule prescribes the procedure for altering, scheduling or rescheduling of any Scheduled Areas in any states. Accordingly, the

President may at any time by order: i) direct that the whole or any specified part of a Scheduled Area shall cease to be a Schedule Area or a part of such an area; ii) increase the area of any Scheduled Area in a state after consultation with the Governor of that State; iii) alter the boundaries of a State on the admission into the Union or the establishment of a new State, declare any territory not previously included in any State to be, or to form part of, a Scheduled Area; iv) rescind, in relation to any state of States, any order or orders made under this paragraph, and in consultation with the Governor of the State concerned, make fresh orders redefining the areas which are to be Scheduled Areas.

The above-mentioned provisions imply that the President is the authority to declare any area as a Scheduled Area or renounce a Scheduled Area or part of a Scheduled Area as a non-Scheduled Area in consultation with the Governor of the concerned State. Under the provisions of the Fifth Schedule, the Governors of the States having Scheduled Areas are empowered to exercise extensive power and functions to discharge for the administration and control of the Scheduled Areas. The Governors of these states are required to submit a report to the President annually or whenever so required by the President regarding the administration of the Scheduled Areas in that State and the executive power of the Union shall extend to the giving of directions to the respective States for the administration of the Scheduled Areas (Part A, Para 3). The Governor is authorised to direct the State government by public notification not to apply any Act of Parliament or of the State Legislature to a Scheduled Areas or apply it subject to exceptions or modifications (Part B, Para 5(1)). The Fifth Schedule assigns special responsibilities to the Governors for ensuring peace and good governance in the Scheduled Areas. For this, as per the provision 120 Federalism and Decentralization under Para 5(2), the Governor can make regulations in the Scheduled Areas particularly for the following purposes: i) to prohibit or restrict the transfer of land by or among the members of Scheduled Tribes in such areas, ii) to regulate the allotment of land to members of the Scheduled Tribes, iii) to regulate the carrying on of business as money-lenders by persons who lend money to members of the Scheduled Tribes in such area Another significant provision for the administration and control of the Scheduled Areas and Scheduled Tribes is the establishment of a Tribes Advisory Council (TAC). Under Para 4 in part B of the Fifth Schedule, each state having Scheduled Areas has the constitutional obligation to constitute a Tribes Advisory Council.

The President may also direct any state having Scheduled Tribes but not Scheduled Areas to create a Tribes Advisory Council consisting of not more than twenty members of whom nearly three-fourth shall be the representatives of Scheduled Tribes in the State Assembly. As per the provisions are given in Para 4(2) of the Fifth Schedule, the primary duty of the Tribes Advisory Council is to advise the State Government on matters related to the welfare and advancement of Scheduled Tribes in the state or on any matter which may have been referred to them by the Governor.

Besides, under Article 339 (1) of the Constitution, the President may also appoint a Commission to report on the administration of the Scheduled Areas and welfare of the Scheduled Tribes in the states. As it was obligatory to appoint such Commission at the end of the first ten years of the implementation of the Constitution, the First Scheduled Areas and Scheduled Tribes Commission was appointed in 1960, with U.N. Dhebar as the Chairman to address the overall situation of the tribals, including the issue of land alienation in the tribal areas. The Commission submitted its report in 1961. And in 2002, the Second Commission was set-up under the Chairmanship of Shri Dileep Singh Bhuria (The Bhuria Commission) to review the constitutional mechanisms for the welfare and development of Scheduled Tribes. Thus, the Fifth Schedule of the Constitution created an institutional mechanism in the form of the Tribes Advisory Council for the administration of the Scheduled Areas and the Scheduled Tribes in different parts of the country other than the four North-Eastern States of Assam, Meghalaya, Mizoram and Tripura. The four States of North-East are excluded from the purview of the Fifth Schedule since they are administered separately under the scheme of the Sixth Schedule."[3]

[iv] According to Article 244 of the constitution the sixth schedule lays down special provisions for the protection of the interest and cultural identities of the hill tribe of North. The most important provisions of the VI schedule is certain of the Autonomous District Councils. While tribals of some of the North-Eastern states have the Autonomous District Councils, Arunachal Pradesh, Nagaland and greater part of Mizoram do not have this.

"According to Dr. Ambedkar, the tribal people of Assam differed from the tribals of other areas. As for the latter, they were more or less Hinduised, more or less assimilated with the civilization and culture of the majority of the people in whose midst they lived. As for the former, their roots were still in their own civilization and their own culture. They had not adopted either the modes or the manners of the Hindus who surrounded them. Their laws of inheritance, their laws of marriage, Custom, etc. were quite different from that of Hindus. He felt that the position of the tribals of Assam was somewhat analogous to that of the Red Indians (Now referred to as American Indians) in the United States, who are a Republic by themselves in that country, and were regarded as a separate and independent people. He agreed that Regional and District Councils have been created to some extent on the lines which was adopted by the United States for the purpose of the Red Indians.This schedule provides for two kinds of governing units in the Tribal Areas: the Autonomous District Councils and the Autonomous Regions.

A. The Governor has the Power to include, exclude or diminish any of these areas or define their boundaries [S 1]. B. There shall be a District Council for Each Autonomous District comprising not more than 30 members and a Regional council for the Autonomous Regions. C. The powers of administration shall be vested in these Districts and Autonomous Council [S 2(4)]. The Governor shall be entitled to make rules for the constitution of the Councils, its Composition, and terms of office, appointment of officers and staff and procedure and conduct of business. a. The Elected members of the council shall have normal term of five years [S 2(6&7)]. b. The District and the Regional Council have the power to make rules in respect of lands other than the Reserved Forest, management of forest, other than reserved forest, use of canal or water courses for agriculture, Regulation of jhum other forms of shifting cultivation, establishment of village or town committees, appointment or succession of chief or headmen, inheritance of property, marriage and divorce and social customs with the prior approval of the government [S 3]. c. The District and the Regional Council are also empowered to constitute village councils for trial or suits and cases between the except those, which has been excluded otherwise. They may similarly prescribe and lay down their procedures for trial and enforcement of their decisions [S 4]. d. The Governor may delegate the additional powers under the code of civil procedures and code of criminal procedures. e. The District Councils may establish and manage primary schools, agriculture, animal husbandry and other community projects [S 6]. f. They have their own district and their regional funds and may assess and collect land revenue and impose taxes, grant licenses and leases for minerals [S 9], make regulations for control of money lending and trading by non-tribals [S 10], Regulate publications [S 11], etc. g. The Governor has the powers to direct the exclusion or modification of any act of the State Legislature of the Arunachal Pradesh, Assam, Manipur, Mizoram, Meghalaya, Nagaland, Tripura relating to the consumption of non-distilled alcoholic liquor [S 12, 12A to 12B]. The Council shall prepare their Annual financial Statement and the same shall be placed before the Commissions to enquire State Legislature [S 13]. h. The Governor has powers to appoint Commissions to enquire into the affairs of any Council [S 15] annul or suspend any office acts or resolutions and dissolve the Council and direct general elections subject to the prior approval of the State Legislature [S 16]"[4]

(v)The Lok Sabha unanimously passed two Constitution Amendment Bills. The first Bill empowers the Government to set up a separate National Commission for the Scheduled Tribes, While the second bill seeks to protect the rights of the non-tribals in the newly –elected Bodo Territorial Council (BTC) in Assam."The framers of the Indian Constitution were concerned about the problems of tribes. Article 32 of the Constitution provides the right to Constitutional remedies. All the Articles discussed in the content are in favour of tribe preservation, upliftment, safeguard and socio-economic development. The framers of the Constitution wanted to build an egalitarian Indian society through these Articles. Both the Central government and State government have the responsibility to take measure for wellbeing of tribes and towards that end create social consciousness. Today, tribal people are not even able to demand their rights due to poor response of the authorities. Moreover when they approach the authorities to claim their rights, they are asked to produce certain documents which they generally do not have and thus they fall prey to corruption. Consequently the fate of the tribal people is yet to be up to the mark despite there being a rich legislation because of poor or improper implementation."[5]

The administration of scheduled areas in states are dealt with in schedule fifth, the sixth schedule deals with the Tribal areas in Assam, Meghalaya, Tripura and Mizoram. Tribal areas are to be administered as autonomous districts.

"These autonomous districts are not outside the executive authority of the state concerned but provision is made for the creation of District Councils and Regional Councils for the exercise of certain legislative and judicial functions. These councils are primarily representative bodies and they have got the power of law-making in certain specified fields such as management of a forest other than a reserved forest, inheritance of property, marriage and social customs, and the Governor may also confer upon these councils the power to try certain suits or offences. These Councils have also the power to asses and collect land revenue and to impose certain specified taxes. The laws made by the Councils shall have, however, no effect unless assented to the Governor.

With respect to the matters over which the District and Regional Councils are thus empowered to make laws, Acts of the State Legislature shall not extend to such Areas unless the relevant District Council so directs by public notification. As regards other matters, the President with respect to a Central Act and the Governor with respect to a State Act, may direct that an Act of Parliament or of the State Legislature shall not apply to an modifications as he may specify in his notification.

These Councils shall also process judicial power, civil and criminal, subject to the jurisdiction of the High Court as the Governor may from time to time specify."[6]

CHAPTER SIX

INDIAN TRIBAL CULTURE: AN ECONOMIC PERSPECTIVE

Introduction

The first image that comes to mind when we think about tribal people is a picture of half-naked men and women holding a weapon like a spear or an arrow while chatting in a coded language. There were communities still preserving their old values, rituals, and beliefs at a time when the majority of humanity was keeping up with global progress. Tribal people in India are frequently referred to as Adivasis. They have historically been India's most at-risk community. Tribes are uneducated, underdeveloped, and frequently lack access to basic services like healthcare and education. The tribal groups of India have grown to be who they are in close proximity to the natural resources that have shaped their social structures, religious beliefs, economic systems, and modes of production. They have grown symbiotic relationships with their immediate surroundings over time. For them, land serves as a symbol of their cultural identity and existence rather than just a means of subsistence. One of the most important socioeconomic sub-systems is the economy. In order to do social work in tribal India, one must have a thorough understanding of the structure and dynamics of the economic system, as the majority of the issues affecting tribal welfare are intertwined with them. It's interesting to note that economic arrangements in tribal and non-tribal communities all around the world differ significantly from one another. Additionally, India's tribal economies are at various phases, from food collection to industrial labour.

The forest holds a key place in the economy. The forest heavily influences the tribal way of life from conception to death. Despite the protections provided by the Indian constitution to the tribal community, they continue to be the most underdeveloped ethnic group in India. The adivasi worldview of resource exploitation is diametrically opposed to the policy of liberalisation and the new state conceptions of resource usage, and this gap has only become wider with the introduction of globalization's market-oriented philosophy of development. Up until now, people who already have an advantage in education and talent have benefited from globalisation. For the tribal people, globalisation means higher costs, less job stability, and inadequate access to healthcare. Rapid technological development, unmatched economic and political power, and the rise of neo-colonialism through the G-8 and other agencies like the IMF, WB, and IBRD have all contributed to favourable conditions for the theft and extraction of natural resources from tribal people's ecologically vulnerable territories. This area is home to all of the large steel mills, BALCO, the majority of river basin development plans and hydropower projects, a network of forestry-related and ancillary enterprises, and an increasing number of highly polluting industries. Even though there is a lot of industrial activity in the central Indian tribal belt, there is very little native employment in contemporary businesses. Tribal people are made to coexist with alien capitalist relationships and traditions. They are compelled to enter the increasing, precarious, unstable, low-paying, and destitute labour market.

Economic Change in Tribal India

India's tribal economy are undergoing changes. Their interactions with various exogenous forces resulted in change in them. They use contemporary technology and techniques, make adjustments to the dynamics of the modern economy, and are aimed toward accomplishing the objective of development. The economic makeup and roles of tribes in India have changed as a result of a variety of reasons. In response to forces of modernization, the major tribes of India are experiencing the following five interconnected phases of economic change:

1. Occupational Change: Modern Jobs Replacing Traditional Jobs: Tribal economies are straightforward primary producers, and the majority of the population relies on the land and the forest for a living. Tribal people are altering their economic activity in response to state and federal government initiatives. Numerous tribespeople have also become more

and more involved in modern vocations. Some tribes gradually transition from their traditional shifting farming to settle cropping because it is less lucrative and less harmful to the environment. Several other tribes who have traditionally hunted are now engaging in horticulture as well as their customary activity. As we saw in the last section, many tribe members have taken up white collar employment as a result of educational advancement. Some people who were marginalised in agriculture started working as agricultural or industrial wage earners as a result.

2. From Sustenance to Commercialization: The tribal economies have been persistent and stagnant for a very long time. The production and acquisition of commodities and services by the tribal people were focused on meeting domestic consumption needs. There wasn't much of a surplus with them. Both the desire to make a profit and the desire to save were absent from them. Due to their greater involvement with the nontribal economy, this has significantly changed. The growth of commercial aptitude among various tribes in India has been facilitated by the development of physical infrastructure, particularly roads, transport, and communication facilities in tribal areas, exposure to agricultural extension agencies, etc. Many of them now cultivate vegetables or gather items from the forest to sell in the neighborhood market. Food crops primarily intended for home consumption have given way to commercial crops like potatoes, green vegetables, and fruits that are intended for markets, changing the cropping patterns in the tribal communities.

3. Market commoditization and integration: Due to their limited interaction, tribal people were, for the most part, beyond the purview of national and international market pressures. However, the market forces have made their way into tribal communities via the roads, modes of transportation, and lines of communication, as well as via the efforts of banks, cooperatives, businesses, money lenders, etc. They are being assimilated into the market's network structure. The market forces have an impact on their daily economic activity. The variations in pricing levels have an impact on them. They view the products and services as commodities that can be bought or sold. Many of them have mastered the selling, buying, and haggling techniques found in contemporary markets.

4. Barter to Monetary Exchange: One of the most significant changes in India's tribal economy is the introduction of money. Simply put, it is the transition from traditional barter exchange to financial transactions. The majority of the tribes were not aware of or did not use money as a unit of measure for the worth of their goods and services in economic transactions. Money has become the most widely used form of exchange for goods and services in tribal India as a result of the contact of the tribal people with the outside economy through periodic markets and the formation of cooperative and commercial banks and organisations. In the tribal economy, monetization and market penetration reinforce one another.

5. Proletarianisation Depeasantisation and Impoverishment: Tribes' economies have been in decline as a result of economic integration, market penetration, commoditization, and commercialization. The economic downfall of tribal people has occurred as a result of widespread tribal debt, land alienation, landlessness, and/or forced labour. The poverty rate in India's tribal communities has increased as a result of economic modernization, not as a result of it. Although there are constitutional provisions for their protection, non-tribal merchants, moneylenders, and occasionally forest officials have taken advantage of tribal people and have stripped them of their property and means of subsistence. Unfortunately, tribal people still represent the most economically disadvantaged inhabitants of our democratic republic notwithstanding the execution of the Ten Five Plans. Tribal leaders and the masses have used innovative movements and fights to address their economic issues. The fragile, unsophisticated tribal economies are becoming more and more connected with the global economy as a result of new economic policy, with far-reaching effects on people's livelihoods and living situations.

- **Impact of Globalization on Tribals**

The tribal people are a component of Indian society, hence general issues with modernising or consciously changing Indian society also apply to them. The issue is the nature and character of this specific category, which the tribal peoples represent as a special case within this larger framework. In India, policies and programmes for tribal development made the assumption that all tribal people will advance and become a part of the "mainstream." This just took place symbolically. Due to planned tribal development, tribal people have begun to stratify along secular lines, and only a tiny portion of them have been able to benefit from development programmes.

1. Tribals being uprooted: It is estimated that since independence, more than 16 million people—of whom 40% are tribal—have been uprooted from their villages as a result of the building of more than 1500 significant irrigation development projects.
2. Tribal Land Alienation: Land is a crucial element in the growth of a tribe. It takes up their source of support. But the globalisation trend has cut indigenous people off from their source of support.
3. Problems with Debt: Due to insufficient resources for their way of life, the global economy has overextended the tribal people with numerous loans. Tribal communities are in debt as a result of their low levels of education, low purchasing power, and lack of means for working for a living. Tribal people are forced into a state of extreme poverty by their debt.
4. Intellectual Property Rights in Danger: In the age of globalisation, it appears that the existence of IPR in agrarian communities is dwindling.
5. Extinction of primitive tribal culture: Globalization's ethos has had an impact on tribal peoples' cultural status in addition to their socioeconomic circumstances.
6. Privatization of PSUs: Disinvestment or privatisation is one method of globalisation in India. The tribal belt's profit-making businesses, including BALCO, have been privatised. PSEs in the tribal belt provided native people with employment and a means of subsistence. The tribal people have been negatively impacted by the privatisation of these businesses, which has also upset the regional industrialization balance.

Recommendation and Findings

• The new economic policies have a significant impact on the lives of adivasis, whose rights to access to natural resources, opportunities for livelihood, primary health care, protection from atrocities and violations of human rights, and the right to maintain their traditional and customary practises are all seriously threatened as a result of the changes in laws and policies.

- Disinvestment or privatisation is one method of globalisation in India. In order to increase revenue and close the budget gap while also increasing efficiency, many public sector businesses are being sold to the private sector. The tribal people will suffer if these businesses are privatised, and the industrialization of the region will be out of balance.
- The alienation of tribal land was made possible by the new industrial agenda. As a result, tribal lands are alienated for a variety of purposes, including the building of dams, mining operations, the establishment of wildlife sanctuaries, the building of government infrastructure, and encroachments by non-tribal people.
- Adivasis have been uprooted and forced to live on the periphery of globalisation, and non-tribal people have indirectly and on a huge scale destroyed natural resources for industrial uses.
- Issues like unemployment and poverty among indigenous people are caused by the changing environment and customs. They are compelled to work as bonded or farm labourers. They also relocate to distant locations in pursuit of employment.

Conclusion

Tribes are distinct from Indian society while also being a part of it. Tribal peoples have been isolated from the main stream of the nation's socioeconomic growth due to centuries of exploitation and repression. The indigenous people of our nation are known as the tribal population. They represent the most vulnerable group in our society, maintaining their traditional values, practises, and beliefs while living in a natural, pollution-free environment remote from modern culture. The benefits of globalisation have so far gone to people who already have an advantage in terms of education and skills, greater access to markets, and ownership of assets that can be used as collateral for loans. To ensure proper legitimization of tribal voices, identities, cultures, collective human rights, and contextual issues in the age of globalisation and the digital divide, it is crucial for both the tribal and non-tribal populations of India to close the representation gap. India needs to reconsider and revise its definition of development in order to include the discussion of inclusive development because it aspires to become a developed nation. Without a doubt, this also involves the welfare of tribal society, which is marginalised. The mistrust between tribal communities and the government is growing as a result of tribal resentment.

CHAPTER SEVEN

NORTH-EAST INDIAN TRIBAL PEOPLES: ISSUES AND PROSPECTS

Introduction:

This article examines the issues facing the tribal people in India's northeast and offers some answers. From a geopolitical standpoint, northeast India is crucial for India's security. Many tribes have their home in northeast India. In India, tribes are typically referred to as Adivasis, meaning "indigenous people" or "original dwellers." The British government followed an isolationist policy to protect the tribal communities from external influences. During the post-independence period, the government followed the same path as that of the British, and additional provisions were added to the Indian Constitution to safeguard the rights of the tribals of this region. The Central and State governments have passed progressive laws, programs, and plans to develop and empower scheduled tribes. Since India's independence, the indigenous peoples of the north-eastern region have not made any significant advancement compared to their counterparts in other areas and continue to lag far behind regarding infrastructural facilities and all human development parameters. Therefore, under these situations, efforts should be made on the part of governments to improve the overall socio-economic situation in the north-east. Expand job opportunities for educated young people by fostering an atmosphere that would attract IT firms and BPOs to the state's residents. Overall, the government cannot fix the issue on its own; community involvement and NGO involvement are crucial. People should be encouraged to get involved in the regional development process, and the government should work to enhance its governance and administrative delivery systems.

Northeast India refers to the geographical region comprising the states of Assam, Manipur, Meghalaya, Nagaland, Tripura, Arunachal Pradesh, Mizoram and Sikkim. These eight States cover an area of 2,62,189 sq. km. constituting 7.98 per cent of the country's total geographical area[1]. This region is connected to mainland India through a small passage known as the Siliguri Corridor or the Chicken's Neck[2]. It was only seen as a periphery that tribal groups populated with different racial and cultural characteristics were severely or not governed. Even after the end of colonialism, this idea persisted, giving Indian leaders' imaginations a specific colour for a while.

As the intersection of South Asia, South-East Asia, and East Asia, North East India is strategically significant. The international borders of the North-East measure 1,126 km with China, 489 km with Bhutan, 1,643 km with Myanmar, and 1187 km with Bangladesh. The hills and basins of the area occupy an area of 90,160 sq. km., or nearly 60% of the entire region[3]. They are a mixture of high mountain ranges, plateaus, and low hills. In West Bengal, just 2% of the region's boundaries are connected to the rest of India[4]. The region's international borders are closed, and its economic contacts with its neighbors are limited due to insurgency and tense relations.

North-East During the British Period:

For further colonial purposes, the north-eastern region of British India acted as a "frontier region" governed by the Bengal province until 1894[5]. To prevent political influence from the outside world, they isolated this area. They split the hilly regions into two groups depending on their levels of development and accessibility: Excluded areas and Partially Excluded Areas. The North-East Frontier Tracts, the Naga Hills, the Lushai Hills districts, and the North Cachar Hills subdistrict of the Cachar district were categorised as the Excluded Areas. In contrast, the Garo Hills district, the Mikir Hills, the British portions of the Khasi, and the Jaintia Hills district, except Shillong Municipality and Cantonment, were categorised as Partially Excluded Areas[6]. The Inner Line Regulation was implemented, limiting British subjects' access to the territories covered by the last category. The government did not want to permit the plains people to expand their trading operations over the Line since it would make it very difficult for them to collect taxes there. Additionally, by limiting its citizens' access, the government lessened the dangers to their lives posed by tribal assaults.

These limitations were not present in the Partially Excluded Areas. The Partially Excluded Areas tribes were more developed than the Excluded Areas tribes. However, some limitations were placed on these places for the inhabitants of the plains. The excluded territories were directly under British administrative control, and the partially excluded areas received a limited representative system.

North-East During the post-independence Period:

The post-independence government's strategy followed the same administrative structure, and additional provisions were added to the Indian Constitution. When Pandit Jawaharlal Nehru, our nation's first prime minister, established the North-East Frontier Agency (NEFA) in 1951, this region received particular attention. However, after the 1962 Indo-China border conflict[7], the area attracted the serious attention of Indian officials. This battle altered the Indian state's policy view of the region. The Constitution's framers granted autonomy under the Sixth Schedule in recognition of the substantial differences between the north-eastern region's way of life and that of the rest of the nation. Similar to this, the region's administrative structure was gradually reorganised with the creation of the States of Nagaland (1963) and Meghalaya (1972), the grant of Arunachal Pradesh and Mizoram statehood in 1987, and the elevation of Manipur and Tripura from Union Territories to States in 1972[8]. Following the extensive reorganisation of the area in 1972, the North Eastern Council (NEC) was established as a regional organisation to serve as a platform for inter-State cooperation, regional planning, and integrated development of the region to prevent intra-regional imbalances. Sikkim, which joined India in 1975, has been a part of NEC since 1992 as its eighth unit. In 2001, the Department of Development of the North-Eastern Region (DONER)[9] was established as an independent Department of the Union Government. Both NEC and DONER, which fall under the DONER umbrella, contribute to regional planning and development. In the 1990s, the Indian government launched its "look-east" strategy, which aims to boost the economies of the neighboring East Asian nations and India's north-eastern region. The Look East Policy was renamed as the "Act East Policy" [10]by Prime Minister Narendra Modi and the NDA administration due to their commitment to this area.

Many tribes have their home in northeast India. More than 200 indigenous communities exist. Tribes in North East India descended from Tibeto-Burmese, proto-Austrioloids, and specific Indo-Mongoloid ethnic groupings. Many of these tribes originated in China and Southeast Asia, which explains why they share a lot of cultural traits with the populations on the other side of the international boundary. As a result, they have a cultural connection with the nearby nations of Bangladesh, China, Nepal, Bhutan, and Nepal. The tribes of northeast India can be divided into two primary groups: the plain tribes residing in Assam's valley regions, namely the tribes of the Brahmaputra Valley[11], and the hill tribes living in the mountainous areas of Arunachal Pradesh, Mizoram, Meghalaya, and Nagaland. Differences between the two groups point to cultural traits. Up to the British conquest, most hill tribes lived in isolation. However, the tribes of the plains have coexisted with other non-tribal populations. Since the beginning of time, there has been a lot of cultural exchange between the tribes and other nearby societies.

Demographically, scheduled tribes are more abundant in Meghalaya, Mizoram, Nagaland, and Arunachal Pradesh hills than in the valleys of Assam, Manipur, and Tripura. In India, scheduled tribes make up just 8.6% of the population, and there are 645 recognised tribal groupings as of the 2011 census. In 2011, the total population of the scheduled tribes in the north-eastern states of India was 13%. Mizoram had the most significant percentage of scheduled tribes in its population in 2011, followed by Nagaland, Meghalaya, Arunachal Pradesh, Manipur, and Tripura[12].

Fig-1: Tribal Population In the North-East Region: 2011 Census-

Sl. No.	N.E. States	Total Population	ST Population	Percentage of ST Population
1	Mizoram	10,97,206	10,36,115	94.43
2	Nagaland	19,78,502	17,10,973	86.48
3	Meghalaya	29,66,889	25,55,861	86.15
4.	Arunachal Pradesh	13,83,727	9,51,821	68.79
5.	Manipur	28,55,794	11,67,422	40.88
6.	Tripura	36,73,917	11,66,813	31.76
7.	Sikkim	6,10,577	2,06,360	33.80
8.	Assam	3,12,05,576	38,84,371	12.45

Source: Census report 2011, available at https://censusindia.gov.in/census.website/

Tribal Population In the North-East Region: 2011 Census

Among seven north eastern states, Assam had 12.45%, Arunachal Pradesh 68.79%, Manipur 40.88%, Meghalaya 86.15%, Mizoram 94.43%, Nagaland 86.48% and Tripura had 31.76% and Sikkim had 33.80% scheduled tribes population. Presently, in Assam 15 scheduled tribes living in the autonomous districts of Karbi Anglong and North Cachar Hills and 14 scheduled tribes in the State including the Bodoland Territorial Area District and excluding those autonomous districts. In Arunachal Pradesh 16, in Manipur 34, in Nagaland 5, in Meghalaya 17, in Mizoram 15 and in Tripura 19 scheduled tribes are living (Fig:1).

Meaning of Tribals:

In India, tribes are typically referred to as 'Adivasis', meaning "indigenous people" or "original dwellers." According to the Oxford Dictionary, a tribe is a racial group that is bound by language and customs and lives as a community under one or more chiefs. It is important to note that no one criterion has been used to separate the population into tribal and non-tribal. As the British arrived in India, the concept of tribes started to take shape. The 'Adivasis' are classified as scheduled tribes under the Indian Constitution. The Indian Constitution's Article 366 (25) defines the phrase "scheduled tribes." According to Article 366 (25), and Article 342 of the Indian Constitution, scheduled tribes are those communities that have been designated as such by the President of India either through an initial public announcement or through a subsequent amending Act of Parliament[13]. Following consultation with the relevant state governments, the President of India issued a notified order specifying the first scheduled tribe of a given state or UT. The criteria used to designate a group of people as Scheduled Tribes include evidence of primitive features, a distinctive culture, geographic isolation, reluctance to interact with the general public, and backwardness.

Constitutional Provisions:

The main objective of the Indian Constitution regarding the tribal communities is not to disrupt the harmony of tribal life but to work for their advancement and integrate them into the national democratic setup. It does not seek to force anything on them but instead promotes their integration into the national democratic system. The tribal groups and places of India, particularly the north-eastern region, were given a unique role in the new federal structure of Independent India. There are several protections for the welfare of the indigenous people in the Indian constitution. Following the requirements of the Indian Constitution, they fell into the Scheduled Tribes (ST) category. The article numbers 14, 15, 15(4), 16(4), 46, 244(1), 275(1), 330, 332, 335, 340, 342, 5th and 6th Schedule of our Constitution provided some provisions related to the tribals[14].

They are entitled to several constitutional protections that guarantee their social, economic, and political safety. Article 15(4) makes specific allowances for the progress of other disadvantaged groups, including Schedule Tribes. Contrarily, Article 16 guarantees equal access to public work possibilities for all facets of society, including STs. Additionally, they are given a reserve in all elected bodies at all levels of government. The National Commission for Scheduled Tribes was also established under Article 338A to monitor the efficient use of the STs' current protections. The Commission oversees the planning process for the holistic development of STs and conducts investigations into complaints about the infringement of STs' rights. According to Article 244(1) of the Indian Constitution, Scheduled Areas are those the President has proclaimed by order throughout India's nine states and are described in the Fifth Schedule[15]. These locations were chosen primarily due to their geographic extent, economic backwardness, and prevalence of indigenous populations. The fifth schedule does not include Assam, Meghalaya, Mizoram, or Tripura. Article 244(2) of the Indian Constitution provides for the administration of these states through Autonomous District Councils (ADCs), under the Sixth Schedule, to serve the needs of the local indigenous community[16]. According to Article 275(1), some states are also given grants from the Union for the welfare of tribal people and the upgrading of the state's scheduled areas' administrative structure. These grants are distributed according to the state's ST population as a percentage of all Indian tribal people. These funds, which are given in addition to the standard Central Assistance to State Plans, are provided to states for pre-defined programmes focused on the welfare of STs[17].

Governments' Initiatives:

The Central and State governments have passed progressive laws, programmes, and plans for the advancement and emancipation of scheduled tribes. The following discussion touches on a few of the potential development plans.

Autonomous District Councils:

Tribes in the north-eastern area that live on hills have rich cultures and traditions. Under the jurisdiction of the Sixth Schedule, some Autonomous District Councils (ADCs) were established to safeguard this area's distinctive culture. Under the Manipur (Hill Areas) District Councils Act, 1971, six more ADCs have been found in Manipur, in addition to the councils listed in the sixth schedule. These councils oversee training on effective local self-governance techniques and guarantee that their traditions and way of life are preserved. They have the authority to create laws and regulations for local issues, including the building or maintaining elementary schools, hospitals, fisheries, roads, and waterways, among other things. They can also collect revenue for efficient management of their region and hold trials in some criminal situations. Assam's North Cachar Hills and Karbi Anglong[18] ADCs have been granted more freedom to draught regulations regarding secondary education, sanitation, and public health issues. Similarly, the Bodoland Territorial Council may use its authority to enact legislation governing tourism, agricultural education, animal husbandry, and other fields.

Enactments of Laws:

The Scheduled Tribes and Other Traditional Forest Dwellers (Recognition of Forest Rights) Act, 2006, was implemented by the Ministry of Tribal Affairs.[19] The legislation intends to acknowledge the traditional rights of tribal and other social groups reliant on the nation's forested regions and rights passed down through generations. It was put in place to safeguard these people's traditional ways of life and livelihoods, which were in danger since their land rights weren't officially recognised. Further, the government of India changed the Land Acquisition Bill to the Right to Fair Compensation and Transparency Bill, 2012[20]. It introduced a specific clause for the tribals to preserve their land rights. The Prohibition of Employment as Manual Scavengers and their Rehabilitation Act, 2013 was also enacted by the Indian Parliament[21]. The purpose of this Act is to end the cruel practise of manual scavenging and to rehabilitate all former manual scavengers who are members of scheduled tribes.

Tribal Sub Plan (TSP):

The TSP was created to ensure specific planning for the nation's tribal regions. It is managed as a component of the state's broader strategy, emphasising the indigenous populace more strongly. The TSP seeks to protect tribal people from exploitation while raising their standard of living. To guarantee the effective operation and seamless coordination of TSP, Integrated Tribal Development Projects (ITDPs) were established at the block or tehsil level during the Fifth Five Year Plan, comprising more than 50% of the ST population. The Vanbandhu Kalyan Yojana was introduced as a Central Sector Scheme in 2014 in response to the TSP's requirement for monitoring and the goal of covering every tribe in the nation[22]. The VKY is a goal-oriented strategy that uses efficient resource convergence to guarantee that STs receive benefits from current state and central government initiatives in a targeted manner.

Support to Voluntary Organizations:

To create a supportive environment for the socio-economic uplift of the Scheduled Tribes, the Indian government also supports nonprofit organisations that assist in putting government welfare programmes into action and filling service gaps in tribal areas, particularly in education, health, and livelihood (STs).[23]

Venture Capital Fund:

The Central government created this programme to encourage entrepreneurship among India's population of scheduled tribes, who are focused on innovation and emerging technology. The programme aims to offer hand-holding support to ST Entrepreneurs' new incubation and start-up concepts. The plan gives the entrepreneurs from the scheduled tribes preferential financing so they may build lucrative enterprises while also generating wealth and value for society.

Tribal Research Information, Education, Communication and Events (TRIECE):

Grants are also provided for planning tribal festivals, research and evaluation initiatives, seminars and workshops, and publishing literature about tribal concerns. It has been acknowledged that centres of excellence should be involved in developing long-term, policy-oriented research studies for the country's tribal development[24].

Fellowship and Scholarship for Education:

Schedule tribe students at the pre-matric and post-matric levels are eligible for fellowships and scholarships. They are also suitable for scholarships for further education in India and abroad for M. Phil, Ph.D., professional courses, and post-doctoral studies in recognised world-class institutions.

Marketing and Logistics Development:

The Central government launched the Marketing and Logistics Development Scheme to provide financial assistance for promoting North Eastern Tribal products to identify artisans, create markets for their products, mainstream and scale up sales of the NE products, increase incomes of the Tribes of the North East, and facilitate year-round livelihoods for the community.

Model Residential Schools:

The central government started the Eklavya Model Residential Schools (EMRS) programme to give Scheduled Tribes (ST) students in remote areas access to high-quality middle and high-level education. By doing so, they would be able to take advantage of reservations for higher education, professional jobs in government and the public and private sectors, and the best educational opportunities on par with non-ST people.

Support to Tribal Research Institute:

For research and evaluation, preservation and documentation of tribal cultural heritage, indigenous practices, art, and culture, as well as training and capacity building of Panchayati Raj Institution (PRI) representatives, officers, and teachers on Forest Rights Act, Panchayats Extension to Scheduled Areas Act.(PESA)[25], constitutional provisions, and state and federal government programmes for the welfare of tribal people, financial assistance is provided to tribal research institutes of the states under the Support to Tribal Research Institute programme.

Development of Particularly Vulnerable Tribal Groups (PVTGs):

Under the plan, the Indian government provides funding to the relevant States for developing Particularly Vulnerable Tribal Groups (PVTGs) that have been recognized thoroughly while preserving their culture and legacy. This Sub-Scheme is under the Program for the Development of Scheduled Tribes from 2022-2023[26].

Challenges faced by the tribal peoples of the NE India:

Since India's independence, the indigenous peoples of the North East region have not made any significant advancement compared to their counterparts in other regions. Tribal people have different social, political, economic, and ecological levels than others, so the severity of their problems varies. Despite these variations, the indigenous people frequently face the following cases:

1. **Economic Problems:**

Before British domination, the tribal peoples of the north-eastern area had a strong sense of community life. The exchange of products and transactions at weekly marketplaces and fairs was the primary mode of commercial connection. However, the British seized the woods essential to their way of life. Moneylenders alienated them from the land they farmed and placed it under their control by giving loans at exorbitant interest rates and then mortgaging their lands. The indigenous inhabitants of this area were exploited and reduced to pauperism due to debt.

1. **Illiteracy:**

The high frequency of illiteracy and extremely high rate of early dropout among the indigenous population in the area were caused by early child labour, poverty, and a lack of supported schooling. The provision for a stipend for indigenous children's education and reservation in educational institutions, government employment, and other areas remains underutilized. This can be seen from the findings of the census report (2011) indicating the literacy rate of tribes was only 58.96 % as against the literacy rate of total population (72.99 %) with a gap of 14.03 %. As far as the North East Region (NER) is concerned, the STs constitute 56.11 % of the total population. Their literacy rate (76.76%) is lower than that of the total population (78.51 %). The high frequency of illiteracy and extremely high rate of early dropout among the indigenous population in the area were caused by early child labour, poverty, and a lack of supported schooling. The provision for a stipend for indigenous children's education and reservation in educational institutions, government employment, and other areas remains underutilized. This suggests that the north-eastern area is concerned about the educational status of tribes.

2. **Tribal Non-Tribal Assimilation:**

The tribal populations, particularly those in the north-eastern area, have been significantly impacted by India's foremost cultural streams. The distance between tribals and non-tribals has reportedly closed, but modernization and industry have brought new issues. Tribal members uprooted from their homes have not been integrated into the new order. They are thus confronted with a new type of pauperism without a traditional support system. Following the country's 1947 division, waves of immigrants from nearby nations arrived in the region. According to the 2011 Census, the Northeast has 14.9 million migrant people, roughly 33 percent of the region's population. This indicates a 5.0 million increase in migrants from the census of 2001. As a result, the north-eastern area developed into a new centre for individuals of various ethnic and linguistic backgrounds, which made the demographic and cultural environment too complicated for the future.

3. Conflict between Traditional and Modern Forces:

Another significant issue in tribal societies is the struggle between traditional and contemporary forces. The traditional forces work to uphold the status quo, while the modern forces work to encourage change. The former try to throw the traditional structure of society off balance, and the latter seek to prevent it. Therefore, the development in the tribal regions, especially in the north-eastern region, is sluggish.

4. Lack Awareness about Government Scheme:

The Indian constitution includes special clauses and privileges for the indigenous people's social, economic, and educational welfare. The majority of indigenous people are, however, not aware of either constitutional provisions or governmental actions. They are therefore ignorant of the government support programmes that have been set up for them. They occasionally receive poor treatment from government officials. Even, most of them have no bank account.

5. Underdevelopment:

The issue of economic underdevelopment is the second most dangerous threat that faces humanity. Natural resources and minerals are abundant in the northeast. People worked hard as well. But the folks are underprivileged. According to the per capita gross state domestic product (GSDP), the region's population has a much lower living standard than the rest of the nation. In 2004-05, the GSDP of the region at Rs. 18027 was less than the overall state average of Rs. 25968. With the introduction of market based economic reforms this difference in the growth rates increased further. During the period 1990-91 to 2004-05, while the aggregate GSDP of all states increased at the rate of 6% per year, the corresponding figure for the region was 4.4%. Also, the region's growth rate of per capita income at 2.5% was significantly low as compared to the national growth rate of 4% during the same period[27]. Low GSDP is caused by various factors, including geographic isolation, insurgency, and infrastructure constraints.

6. Exploitation of Natural Resources:

Natural resources, including oil and natural gas, food grains, horticultural goods, tea, coffee, and forest products like rubber, medicinal plants, cane, and bamboo, are all abundant in the northeastern area. Half of all the tea produced in India is produced in Assam. However, the region is highly underdeveloped, with per capita income well below the national average. Manipur (36.89%), Arunachal Pradesh (34.67%), and Assam (31.96%) have more significant percentages of people living in poverty than the national average of 21.92%, except for Nagaland (18.88%), Tripura (18.05%), Sikkim (8.19%), Meghalaya (11.87), and Mizoram (20.40%).[28] Before the British arrived, the aboriginal people had unrestricted ownership and management rights over natural resources, including land, forests, etc. But since the advent of plantation cultivation, the indigenous people's way of life has altered. Uncontrolled mining and excessive resource extraction in the north-eastern area present another complicated problem concerning the issue of economic growth. Due to government-led development initiatives in partnership with MNCs and international financial organisations like the World Bank and the Asian Development Bank, the existence of the region's people is in danger.

7. Lack of Governance:

The northeastern region's governance service has proven difficult and unsatisfactory. The most significant barriers to implementing governance in the northeast region include red trapism, corruption, underdevelopment, the autonomy movement, the thread of peace, etc. The area has badly failed to bring about corresponding decent governance. Poverty, employment, and socioeconomic success vary widely across and within states, urban and rural areas, and between males and females.

8. Health and Nutrition:

The public health and nutrition of our country's tribal people and the northeast, in general, are not good. The Indian health industry has seen considerable advancements throughout the years. However, the enormous weight of starvation, infectious illnesses, maternity and child health issues, etc., continues to plague tribal groups, particularly in the north-eastern area. States in the Northeast comprise 4.6% of hospital beds and 7% of hospitals overall. Three states, or 2.4% of all India, namely Arunachal Pradesh,

Assam, and Sikkim, reported having doctors with the necessary credentials. Assam has the most significant percentage among these three states, at 94%.[29] These statistics unmistakably show that the infrastructure, human resources, and administration of the public health system in this region are still insufficient.

9. AFSPA and HR violations:

The Armed Forces Exceptional Powers Act, 1958, often known as the "AFSPA," grants the Army some special powers in any of the troubled regions of the nation and gives its acts legal standing[30]. It grants the Army judicial immunity. The act is allegedly lenient against rebels but harsh on the general populace. In the northeast and Kashmir area, several demonstrations have been against the Act. Manipuri activist Irom Sharmila called for repealing the Act by fasting for 11 years[31]. Due to this, the Act was once more the subject of national attention and discussion. Additionally, it has been argued that the Act is misunderstood and authorises the Army to carry out "atrocities" against the populace. The Naga People's Movement for Human Rights v. Union of India case was heard by the Supreme Court, which upheld the Act's constitutional validity[32]. The Armed Forces Special Powers Act was passed to curb terrorism against the country. Sometimes the armed forces began abusing the legislation and turning violent towards law-abiding civilians who weren't insurgents. As a result, everyday violations of fundamental human rights occur, particularly in troubled areas. The AFSPA has to be changed to prevent the military from killing innocent individuals without a good reason.

10. Drug Addiction:

The use of drugs poses a severe threat to tribal civilization. In tribal society, drinking alcohol is a component of social customs. Their diets are insufficient without alcohol. Most of the money they make is spent on alcohol. Young people in this area are increasingly becoming addicted to other substances like heroin, opium, cannabis, cigarettes, etc., which are more readily available in towns and cities and in large quantities in different regions of the north east. Several factors contribute to the North East's rising drug trade and drug usage. The area was transformed into a haven for drug trafficking for various reasons, like its closeness to the

"Golden Triangle" [33], engagement in international politics, and rebel organisations' reliance on macro funds to maintain their arsenals of weapons and ammunition, etc. In tandem with drug abuse, the HIV/AIDS pandemic has rapidly expanded throughout our area. The adult HIV and AIDS prevalence rates in Manipur and Nagaland are 1.57 percent and 1.2 percent, respectively, according to the Department of AIDS Control, Ministry of Health and Family Welfare, which are much higher than the national average of 0.34 percent. The North East region of India has fewer residents than other Indian states. However, there are 100,000 people there who are HIV and AIDS positive[34]. The North East has the most significant death rate in the nation, and drug-related fatalities have reached an all-time high. Last year, drug poisoning-related mortality in the Northeast increased from 332 to 389, a 14% increase. It's the worst number recorded since records were kept in 1993, and it shows that drug deaths significantly increased while the country was under lockdown due to the COVID epidemic[35]. Drug usage causes twice as many deaths in males as in females.

10. Unemployment:

North East India is where one may observe the negative impacts of unemployment at its worst. The missionaries' contributions to education during the British era were notable, and the northeastern states' high literacy percentage proves this. With 91.58 percent, Mizoram has the second-highest literacy rate, followed by Nagaland (80.11%), Manipur (70.85%), Tripura (87.75%), Assam (73.18%), Meghalaya (75.48%), and Arunachal Pradesh (66.95%).[36] In this location, there are surprisingly few small and medium-sized private firms, which are often responsible for creating jobs in our nation. One's options for finding employment are mostly limited to governmental agencies and the education sector. So there aren't many choices for the individuals there. The government failed to provide opportunity for employment. According to the NER, Nagaland has the second-highest percentage of urban unemployment, at 23.8 percent. In contrast, Tripura has the highest rate at 25.2%.[37]. In this area, more and more young people with degrees are unemployed, evidence that the practical aspect of education has failed. Therefore, in the views of the people there, education is gradually losing importance. The lives of many gifted young people are depressed. The North Eastern youth's attraction to terrorism is a result of unemployment.

Conclusion:

We may conclude that, despite many endeavors, the scheduled tribal communities in the north-eastern region continue to lag far behind regarding infrastructural facilities and all human development parameters. Due to economic activities like industrialization, mining, and a multipurpose project, a substantial percentage of the indigenous groups have been forced out of their natural habitats. Different pieces of regulations, such as the Money Lending (Regulations) Act and Land Transfer Regulations, could not defend them from exploitation. Additionally, the Indian tribal population is negatively impacted by the globalisation process. The assertion of tribal identity based on geography, ethnicity, and languages is the most significant tendency to have evolved in the age of globalisation. Although the socio-economic forces of modernization and growth have undoubtedly benefited particular residents, these advantages have been overshadowed. Involuntary relocation and development-related displacement have severely harmed indigenous people and forced them into the background. The economy has been privatised and made more market-based under the current economic regime, which poses a grave danger to the survival of indigenous groups. Although the socio-cultural changes inside tribal groups have undoubtedly given the tribal members more authority, their sense of cultural identity is under great strain. Therefore, in India's tribal regions, the government should work to preserve the rapidly disappearing tribal customs and culture.

Additionally, efforts should be made to expand job opportunities for educated young people by fostering an atmosphere that would attract IT firms and BPOs to the state's residents. Overall, the government cannot fix the issue on its own; community involvement and NGO involvement are crucial. Both central and state governments should create many economic, social, and political institutions to improve the economic conditions of this region. People should be encouraged to get involved in the regional development process, and the government should work to enhance its governance and administrative delivery systems. Talking with all regional stakeholders is essential to achieve peace and stability in this area, and harsh laws like AFSPA should be abolished. Lastly, while creating policies and carrying them out, the central and state governments should work together.

CHAPTER EIGHT

A STUDY OF WEST BENGAL'S TRIBAL DEVELOPMENT

Introduction

The tribe is an organised, cohesive collection of people who share a common environment, a common tongue, and some fundamental cultural traits. Additionally, it prevents individuals from interacting with others outside of their own group and more strongly binds the members of their own group through shared communal solidarity. Modern anthropologists believe that the tribes that live in a given area or nation and go by different names may not be the only ancestors of the region's prehistoric inhabitants. However, there was a propensity for cultural contact between the Aryans and the indigenous pre-Aryans in ancient India. Or, the current population and the coexistence of the indigenous peoples carried the heritage of the existence of indigenous peoples in the Hindu kingdom of ancient India and later in the Muslim kingdom. In India, the term "adivasi" was used to describe the unique characteristics of an underprivileged community. Again, 70 tribal revolts occurred over the 200-year span of British control, according to V. Raghavaiah's "Tribal Revolts" (Mal Pahari Rebellion 1772, Bhil Rebellion 1818-1831, Singhbhum Rebellion 1831, Kols Rebellion 1831-32, Santhal Rebellion 1855-57 etc.). The existence of the word "tribe" at various points in India's history is demonstrated by all of these tribal movements in British colonial India. However, some members of this underdeveloped community were referred to as "nomadic tribes" or "untouchables" throughout the colonial era. People from this community aspired to once again be considered a part of the "backward class," therefore they founded the Indian French Committee in 1919. During the British colonial era, the new term "Primitive Tribes" was added to the 1931 census. The Indian Constitution, which was influenced by the democratic ideology of the Indian system of government, makes a commitment to establishing equality in society by ensuring justice in the socio-economic and political spheres, as well as equal status and facilities regardless of race, religion, caste, and place of birth. In order to carry out that admirable resolution, the phrase "Scheduled Tribes" has been utilised in the Indian Constitution. Additionally, it has started the process of identifying the tribal communities in India that have lagged behind the mainstream of society in terms of socioeconomic development, political influence, and cultural influence.

Constitutional Provisions and Safeguards for the Tribals in India:

We are aware that India is a sizable country with a sizable population just adjacent to China, where several ethnic groups have lived for a very long period. Indian culture and civilization today are characterised by their unity in variety. It was known to those who drafted our constitution that certain racial or social classes had been denied a variety of rights in our nation. For this reason, the constitutional judge argued that the constitution should include stronger protections for tribal people. Only tribes that have been designated as Scheduled Tribes were covered by the constitutional protections (ST). Following are the divisions of the provisions:

1) Protective provisions

2) Developmental provisions

3) Administrative provisions

4) Reservational provisions

The safeguards for schedule tribes are covered by our constitution's Articles 15, 16, 19, 23, 29, 46, 164, 330, 332, 334, 335, 338, 339, 342, 371(A), 371(B), and 371(C). In addition, we found some constitutional provisions that support the creation of scheduled tribes. The developmental provisions for STs in our constitution are included in articles 15, 16, 19, 46, 275, and 399. A specific administrative structure is becoming necessary in contemporary society due to the growth of special demographic groupings. In this sense, Article 244 of the Indian Constitution deals with the administrative rules for indigenous people. The constitution included some provisions for reservation-based development for scheduled tribes and other economically disadvantaged groups in our nation. There are provisions in the constitution that guarantee STs a place in the legislature, state legislatures, and government jobs, among other things. There are some reservational provisions under articles 15, 243, 330, 332, 334, 335, and 340.

Tribes People in West Bengal: West Bengal is also listed among India's tribally populated regions. The unique information about the tribes in this state is covered in this article. But everyone is more or less aware that many of the hereditary tribes in West Bengal have ancestors from beyond the region. Three categories can be used to roughly classify them. First, there are the indigenous tribes who migrated from Tibet's Mongol branch in the northern Himalayan hills and settled in various regions of Darjeeling and Jalpaiguri in West Bengal many years ago. They include a sizeable portion of Lepcha, Bhutia, Gurung, and Nevar people. Second, Santal, Munda, and Orao are among those who immigrated from Chhotnagpur in Bihar and Orissa and settled in the broad regions of Burdwan, Bankura, Purulia, and Medinipur in West Bengal. Additionally, a portion of the Munda people have lived in the South 24 Parganas for many years. Thirdly, certain tribes with Sino-Mongolian ancestry in the northeastern area bordering India originated in Assam in northeastern India and settled in various regions of North Bengal. But among them are the tribal groups of the Garo, Hadi, and Kachari.

8.6% of India's Scheduled Tribes are spread around the nation, but West Bengal is home to about 5.1% of the nation's overall tribal population, according to the 2011 census. However, it is estimated that native inhabitants make up roughly 75% of West Bengal's total 7 districts. These districts have a combined population of 17.5% in Medinipur, 16% in Jalpaiguri, 11.3% in Purulia, 8.5% in West Dinajpur, 8.2% in Bankura, and 6.2% in North and South 24 Parganas. In several districts of West Bengal, there are 38 Scheduled Tribe communities spread out over a large area, and nine major tribal tribes make up nearly 90% of the state's total number of tribal communities. Santal 54%, Munda 7.5%, Bhumij 7.5%, Kora/Lerbo 3.1%, Kheria 1.8%, Orao 1.4%, Bhutia 1.3%, and Shabar 1.2% are among these tribes.

District wise Tribal Population in West Bengal

District	Total population	Total ST population	Male	Female
North 24 Parganas	1,00,09,781	264,597	134,179	130,418
South 24 Parganas	81,61,961	96,976	49,195	47,781
Bardhaman	77,17,563	489,447	243,581	245,866
Murshidabad	71,03,807	91,035	46,163	44,872
Paschim Medinipur	59,13,457	8,80,015	439,831	440,184
Hugli	55,19,145	229,243	113,249	115,994
Nadia	51,67,600	140,700	71,142	69,558
Purba Medinipur	50,95,875	3,555	1,896	1,659
Haora	48,50,029	11069	5686	5383
Kolkata	44,96,694	10,684	5,729	4,955
Maldah	39,88,845	308,850	155,800	153,050
Jalpaiguri	38,72,846	731,704	365,868	365,836
Bankura	35,96,674	368,690	183,467	185,223
Birbhum	35,02,404	242,484	119,787	122,697
Uttar Dinajpur	30,07,134	162,816	81,831	80,985
Puruliya	29,30,115	540,652	271,803	268,849
Koch Bihar	28,19,086	18,125	9,388	8,737
Darjiling	1,846,823	397,389	197,251	200,138
Dakshin Dinajpur	1,676,276	275,366	138,025	137,341

(Source: Census 2011, Government of India)**District wise distribution of scheduled tribe population in West Bengal**

Central government Sponsored Programmes and Policy for Tribal Development:

The activities carried out by the federal government and several state governments throughout the last decades for the development of scheduled tribes were mostly reflected in the policies stated by the then-prime minister Jawaharlal Nehru. The Twelfth Five-Year Plan states in particular that "the process of development should be all-encompassing, allowing all to participate equally in the growth process and benefiting the Scheduled Tribes directly through various projects and programmes or benefiting from the benefits arising from the general development process." There is no denying that in some instances significant welfare initiatives were established, even though the majority of the projects announced for the welfare of the tribal people are typically symbolic. The infamous Tribes Criminal Act, passed by the former British government, has once more been abolished. The Indian Constitution also grants the status of "Scheduled Tribes" with a number of protections and calls for their protection in government and education. work and related fields. There are tribal peoples who participate in government initiatives (such as the 20-point programmes, work in exchange for food, and the 100-day work requirement under the Mahatma Gandhi Employment Guarantee Act 2005) aimed at reducing poverty and promoting the socioeconomic advancement of disadvantaged groups in India over the years. Currently, various national programmes have been adopted for the welfare of the tribal community, and they are continuously being implemented. For example, the Pradhan Mantri Van Dhan Yojana (2018), Tribal Empowerment under TRIFED (1987), Tribal Healers and Tribal Medicine, National level Tribal Research Institute (2018), and Eklavya Model Residential Schools are social and economic development initiatives launched by the Ministry of Tribal Affairs of the Government of India. In order to provide quality education to tribal students in each block where at least 50% more or 20,000 members of scheduled tribes dwell, the Government of India's Ministry of Tribal Affairs has set a target of opening Eklavya Model Residential Schools by 2022. Currently, there are 226 schools functioning around the nation, with a target of 462 schools in the not too distant future. However, the West Bengal government has decided to open the ninth Pandit Raghunath Murmu Residential School in Bengali using the "Alchiki language" in Bankura, Burdwan, Purulia, West Midnapore, East Midnapore, and Jalpaiguri. Additionally, "Belpahari Residential Girls Schools for Tribals" for women in Belpahari, Krishakbandhu project has granted Rs. 10,000 per year and pension of Rs. 1000 / - per year for 60 year olds all tribal people's in west bengal. All of the afflicted Sundarbans "Aila" ordinary folk, including Jhargram, receive free rice on rations as well.

In particular, Jaharlal Nehru's ideal of a tribal-friendly policy was made possible by the passage of the Scheduled Tribes and Other Traditional Forest Dwellers Act (2006) in 2006. The eviction of tribal peoples from their homes will no longer be as cruel, uncertain, or unearned as it once was in the interest of industrialization or higher development, so this rule is unquestionably necessary for the development of the tribal people. However, India has provided them with the means of land ownership to empower the tribal people in the twenty-first century, which is unquestionably praiseworthy.

Again, every minority community in India is permitted to maintain its own language, script, and culture under Article 29 (1) of the Indian Constitution. The indigenous peoples have not, however, been able to significantly diversify their culture, language, and tradition. However, there is no proof that the state has forcibly forced another language on the tribal people by passing any legislation. However, it has been seen that, in the majority of situations, when a school is founded in a tribal region, the primary language of instruction at that school ends up being the state's official language rather than a tribal language. As a result, the tribal people must take the initiative to boost their self-esteem because their own culture and language are in danger of dying out. However, the tribal culture is currently hoarding a lot of lost. The best illustration of this is how indigenous culture is present throughout huge swaths of western, northern, and southern India. As most of these states are tribal and have institutional arrangements to protect indigenous history and culture through the creation of self-governing districts, tribal cultural heritage in the east, particularly in the north-east, is extremely satisfying. This demonstrates that the different demands of the tribal people may be more easily met when they are organised as a nation.

Tribal Development Schemes in West Bengal: Some important tribal development related government sponsored programme in the state of West Bengal is mentioned below:

Education Schemes:

The Tribal Development Department executes a good number of educational schemes aimed at spreading education among the ST in the State. While there is participation of the Government of India in Post-Matric Scholarship schemes for ST and some special schemes like Central Sector Pre-Matric IX & X ST and up gradation of Merit for Students reading in Classes IX to XII, all other schemes at Pre-Matric level are funded exclusively by the State Government.

Sikshashree:

A new scheme named "Sikshashree" for ST Day scholars studying in classes V to VIII introduced have been recently by merging the existing schemes of Book Grant, Maintenance Grant and Other Compulsory Charges. The objective of the scheme is to provide financial assistance in more transparent manner by providing scholarship through individual bank accounts. The scheme aims to minimize the incidence of drop-out at Pre-Matric stages. Each student is paid @ Rs. 800/- p.a. through his Bank Account only. The annual family income should not exceeding Rs. 2.5 lakh.

Hostel Grant for ST Students Residing in School Attached Hostels:

Total 49,500 ST students have been brought within the fold of this scheme. Each student residing in the Hostel gets hostel grant for 10 months only @Rs.750/- per month. Thus the total amount of grant for each students is Rs.750 x 10 = Rs.7, 500/- only in a year. These hostels attached to the Junior High or Secondary Schools are run and managed by the respective school authorities. This scheme provides opportunity to ST students to grow up in an academic environment. There are 1522 school attached hostels all over the State. The students are advised to communicate with the Hostel Advisory Committee through respective Head of the Institution for admission.

Ashram Hostel:

Ashram Hostels for both ST boy and girl students are set up within the campus of the recognized schools. Students studying in Class I to X usually get admission subject to availability of seats. For maintenance, the students are paid Rs. 750/- per month for the entire academic year. In addition, they are given cots, bedrolls, garments, soap, kerosene by the Department. At present there are 217 such hostels running with 6,234 seat capacity. There is a ceiling of Parents / Guardian's income of Rs.36,000/- p.a. The students intending to stay in Ashram hostels are to apply to their respective Head of the Institution for admission.

Merit Scholarship Schemes for Students Reading in Class ix to xii:

The State Government runs two types of schemes (1) Merit scholarship scheme for ST students' studying in classes IX to XII and (2) Merit Scholarship Scheme for ST girl students studying in classes V to X. All eligible students are to communicate with their respective Head of the Institution / our District level offices to collect forms.

Parents/guardian's Income ceiling	V to X	Quota	IX to XII	Parents/guardian's Income ceiling	Quota
	V to VI – Rs.100/- p.m.		Rs.400/- p.m.		
Rs. 60,920/- p.a.	VII to VIII, Rs.125/- p.m.	1038		Rs. 36,000/- p.a.	410
	IX to X – Rs.150/- p.m.				

Post Matric Scholarship to ST:

The objective of the scheme is to provide financial assistance through bank accounts to the Scheduled Tribe students studying at post matriculation or post secondary stages to enable them to complete their education. The students whose family income does not exceed Rs. 2,50,000/- p.a. are eligible for the scholarship. Since the maintenance allowance for different courses vary widely, the same have been grouped into 4 categories and shown below as I, II, III, IV. The amount of scholarship admissible for each group has been indicated below. Tuition fees and compulsory non-refundable fees are paid as per approved rate of the Govt. institution.

Post Matric Scholarship to ST:

The objective of the scheme is to provide financial assistance through bank accounts to the Scheduled Tribe students studying at post matriculation or post secondary stages to enable them to complete their education. The students whose family income does not exceed Rs. 2,50,000/- p.a. are eligible for the scholarship. Since the maintenance allowance for different courses vary widely, the same have been grouped into 4 categories and shown below as I, II, III, IV. The amount of scholarship admissible for each group has been indicated below. Tuition fees and compulsory non-refundable fees are paid as per approved rate of the Govt. institution.

Up-gradation of Merit for Scheduled Tribe Students:

This scheme has been introduced to remove deficiencies in school subjects and specially for preparing ST students for competitive examinations required for entry into professional courses like Engineering and Medicine and other professional courses. Quota of students under the scheme has been fixed at 72.

Grants	Amount
1. Boarding & lodging charge for 10 months	7,000/-
2. Pocket money for 10 months	2,000/-
3. Books & Stationery	2,500/-
4. Honorarium to Principal, expert & other incidental charges	8,000/-
Total :	19,500/-

Ekalavya Model Residential School:

To provide quality education to Scheduled Tribes Boys and Girls from Class VI to XII, seven 'Ekalavya Model Residential Schools' are functioning in the State in the following Districts (1) Bankura (2) Purulia (3) Burdwan (4) Paschim Medinipur (5) Jalpaiguri (6) Birbhum (7) Dakshin Dinajpur with funds from Government of India and the State Government. These are English Medium Schools under the West Bengal Board of Secondary Education. Each school has a capacity of 420 students. The students who are admitted to these schools are provided with scholarships, free food and lodging etc., Computer education has also been introduced in all the schools from class VI.

Feeder Schools: The English Medium Primary Schools from class I to V are feeding the ST girls and boys students to Ekalavya Model Residential Schools. The students passing Class – V in the feeder schools normally join the Ekalavya Schools in Class VI. The 'Ekalavya Model Schools' under the scheme will eventually come under CBSE Board. Stipends are provided for 1500 boys and girls of these feeder schools in seven districts of this State.

Pandit Raghunath Murmu Residential Schools:

Government of West Bengal decided to construct 9 (nine) residential schools for ST students in the districts of Bankura, Purulia, Burdwan, Paschim Medinipur, Purba Medinipur and Jalpaiguri from Class V-XII in the name of Pundit Raghunath Murmu, eminent cultural reformer and inventor of "Olchiki" script for the Santali language. These are Government sponsored Bengali medium recognized by the West Bengal Board of Secondary Education and West Bengal Council of Higher Secondary Education. Eight Schools have been recognized and started functioning. The Schools are managed by the School Education Department.

Belpahari Residential Girls' schools for Tribals: The residential school for tribal girls at Belpahari, Paschim Medinipur under the management of BCW Department is running. There are 380 tribal girls studying in the school from Class I to Class – XII. All students are provided free food and lodging.

Dr. B R. Ambedkar Medha Puraskar:

A total 625 ST students are selected for award of Dr. B.R. Ambedkar Medha Puraskar on the basis of the result in the X –Standard examinations conducted by West Bengal Board of Secondary Education, the West Bengal Madrasa Board, ICSE and CBSC. The meritorious students of each district get the award. The prize consisting of a Cash Award of Rs. 5000/- and a Certificate of Merit is awarded in a special function.

Special educational development of ST Girls students through distribution of bi-cycles. ST girl students studying in class IX-XII in the LWE affected Blocks of Bankura, Purulia and. Paschim Medinipur Districts were provided bi-cycles during 2012-13. In 2012-13, 9097 nos. of ST girl students were covered. During 2013-14, it was decided to extend the benefit to all ST girl students studying in Class IX to XII in the State. Arrangements have been made for procurement of 60457 no. of bicycles. Distribution completed for nearly 12000 girl students during 2013-14.

Old age Pension Schemes: Under this schemes Scheduled Tribes (ST) beneficiaries coming from below the poverty line families with age of 60 year or above of rural areas including Tea Gardens of West Bengal are eligible to get Rs.1000/- (One thousand) per month as pension. The present quota of the beneficiaries is 130463.

Bi-cycles for Tribal Girls:

The State Government is implementing a scheme of distribution of bi-cycles to the tribal girl students from Class IX to XII in the Left Wing Extremists affected (LWE) blocks in the districts of Paschim Medinipur, Bankura and Purulia. The scheme is aimed at reducing drop out in the schools and to encourage the girl students to continue study. Besides, these bi-cycles will help their families for multipurpose house hold activities. Though objective evaluation of the scheme is yet to be done, however, prima facie it appears that the scheme has a good impact on the girl students. There is huge demand from tribal areas and also from SC dominated backward areas.

Conclusions:

However, despite the fact that there are numerous constitutional clauses and legal safeguards for tribal people in 21st-century India, their position has remained marginalised. The primary cause is the fact that national development and tribe development are not compatible in reality. This has prevented these forest residents from using numerous services and developments provided by the federal and state governments. Therefore, it does not appear that the scheduled tribes are falling behind in their marginal situation. It is believed that each of these laws contributed to the marginalisation of indigenous peoples. Because education was not widely distributed among the native groups. Every tribe naturally sees things simply, but certain egotistical opportunists are exploiting this simplicity to steal the lands of the tribes through a variety of deceitful methods. Additionally, the trend of tribal and indigenous peoples being displaced in the face of increased urbanisation, industrialisation, and globalisation persists even in independent India. The majority of the local administration's officials also come from outside the tribal group. They consequently had the chance to work together with numerous dishonest individuals to lend help. Laws pertaining to the protection of indigenous peoples and laws for common citizens have occasionally been in conflict. The law protecting the interests of certain groups must be subject to the greater general law in order to resolve this disagreement. The Scheduled Tribes and Other Traditional Forest Dwellers Act (Recognition of Forest Rights) is a good example of this (2006). The Land Acquisition Act and the Forest and Wildlife Conservation Act are particularly noteworthy in this regard since they serve the public interest and promote further development. The wellbeing and interests of the tribal people have been sacrificed in the name of the national interest. Finally, suitable actions should be done to protect the citizens of the tribal-Indigenous Peoples and to make them aware of laws, education, and political issues on the basis of the cooperative connection between the Central and State Governments of India. The two governments must be mindful of the indigenous people's cultural, social, economic, and political concerns at the same time. Above all, in order to safeguard these native simple people, the judiciary should provide judgments as impartially as possible without tightening the grip of selfish, dishonest flatterers. As a result, more than in any other way, it will be feasible to integrate them into society.

CHAPTER NINE

STUDY ON WEST BENGAL'S TRIBAL WOMEN'S EMPOWERMENT

Introduction

This Chapter links women empowerment through various means. Social empowerment is a multifaceted empowerment process that helps people gain control over their lives. Empowerment involves awareness; This empowerment can be in various areas, such as social, economic and against violence. This empowerment reflects the stage in the development process of overall development of indigenous women. In addition to household work, family responsibilities, tribal women in India contribute significantly to work. The place of women in tribal communities is quite important. But despite all kinds of economic, social and other changes, tribal women are far behind. This research paper assesses and reviews the status of tribal women empowerment in West Bengal through their social status, education, health, independence, role and position in the workplace. But the important discovery is that women have broken the barrier of being limited to reproduction only and now actively participate in production activities.

Women constitute almost half of the total population of the world. According to the Food and Agriculture Organization of the United Nations, women are the most disadvantaged section of society. But historical background shows that women were given high status in Indian society during Vedic period. Women were known as Ardhangini (half of husband's body). As a mother, wife and sister was in a respected position. Currently they are facing social, emotional, physical and domestic violence. Women empowerment is necessary for economic development as well as society. Empowerment of women is necessary not only for their welfare but also for the development of the country. Empowerment is a multidimensional term. Empowerment of women's status in a society is an extraordinary scenario of social justice. In tribal society women are socially important because economy and family management depend on them and they are hard working. It is important that women contribute to the family income by harvesting forest products like shalpata, palm leaves and fresh produce.

Schedule tribes population in West Bengal:

In West Bengal, Tribal population is 52, 96,963 which male and female are 46,809,027 and 44,467,088 respectively as per Census 2011, which is about 5.8% of the total population of the State. Tribal population of West Bengal constitutes about 5.08% of total Tribal population of the Country. Tribal communities are present in all the Districts of the State. The literacy rate among tribes (58.96%) is found to be far below the overall literacy of the country (74.04%), whereas, in West Bengal, the literacy rate among tribal communities 57.97% is found to be far below the overall literacy of the state 77.08%.

Marriage:

Marital status determines the level of stability of women in any community by indicating whether a woman is married, single or widowed. Child marriage is not allowed in tribal society. The ideal tribal marriage is an arranged marriage between a boy and a girl of an unrelated age. The marriage proposal is first taken from the boy's house to the girl's house. They do not marry into the same clan. In any case, if the blood relationship is detected, they stop the discussion immediately. Girls are preferred and considered in marriage. The practice of bride price is prevalent in tribal societies, as fathers consider a girl as wealth. Because she contributes to the family economy and it eases the wedding expenses.

Widow:

Widow marriage is allowed in tribal society. After the death of the brother, the younger brother can marry the wife of the elder brother, and on the other hand, after the death of the wife, the younger sister of the bride can also be married. Even if there are no children, the husband can remarry again. Divorce is easy in this tribal society if satisfactory proof is produced. In this case, in front of the village chief, the husband takes the iron bangle from his wife's hand and sprinkles water on the shal leaf and tears it into pieces in front of everyone. This is the method of divorce. Husband can claim divorce but the wife cannot. After divorce, the wife can remarry again. Basically tribal society is male dominated. Widowed women who have lost the breadwinner in the family have all the responsibilities of their family on their shoulders. Studies have shown that widows have more decision-making power than others. But they face insecurity and lack of cooperation etc.

Domestic Violence:

Violence or domestic abuse also known as family violence. Patterns of violence or other abuse against women by an individual or by a family member, especially physical and emotional abuse, are seen in tribal societies. This violence takes many forms including social, physical, sexual and psychological. Tribal women are often at high risk of violence. Among them there was exploitation inequality, unequal economic and social status, lack of balanced conductive environment in terms of economic context as well as the traditional concept of free full-time labor of women in the family. Thus the wife had to accept domestic violence from her husband or someone in the family in order to fulfill her family responsibilities. Beatings with hands, sticks or even kicks by husbands were common for tribal wives. Surprisingly, most of the abuses husbands voiced towards their wives included sex. Crimes like sexual abuse, child abuse have been noted. Because of the complexity of economic and social problems coupled with slander and the fear of dirty violence like female feticide and social norms, defensiveness is seen in tribal societies.

Health:

The health of the tribals is not better than the general health due to various reasons. Most of the tribal women prefer to give birth at home. At the time of child birth an old woman of the village works as midwife. That old lady cut the umbilical cord which is planted outside the room. 21 days are observed as an unholy period. Rituals like burying the umbilical cord of the house for the survival of the newborn. Babies were not breastfed in the first days due to blind belief which is extremely harmful for babies. Most women return to work after seven to eight days. Infants were also deprived of exclusive breastfeeding for six months. Women's empowerment is needed to break out of superstitions and bridge gaps in various issues. Infant mortality rate is highest among the tribal population.

Education:

Socio-cultural and health development is universally strengthened through the instrument which is education. Aboriginal women have the highest rate of never going to school. Education is a fundamental right that provides opportunities for socio-economic development. The tribal girl child is deliberately deprived of education, which reduces their chances of future development. Financial constraints, child marriage, motherhood and narrow parental ideas about girls' education are seen in tribal society. Education helps tribal women to fulfill certain social roles. The main purpose of education is to empower women. Namely:

1. Educated women and eradication of illiteracy.

2. Developing self-reliance and confidence.

3. To increase body and sexuality awareness among women.

4. Providing training for income enhancement.

The Panchayat Extension to Scheduled Areas Act 1996:

The Act effectively introduced ashram schools centrally for children from primary to higher secondary level in tribal areas. But trust in education, which is a vehicle for social mobility, has declined because of the poor quality of education in ashram schools.

Tribal education is a priority area in the tribal sub-plan from the Fifth Five Year Plan. Education of ST children is considered important not only because of constitutional obligation, but as an important factor for the overall development of the tribal community.

The National Education Policy 1986 has specified the following subjects -

1. Permission to open primary schools in tribal areas.

2. Curriculum development and development of instructional materials in tribal languages with provision for transition to regional languages at the initial stage.

3. Encouraging ST youth to teach in tribal areas.

4. Ashram schools / residential schools will be established on a large scale in tribal areas. In some states like West Bengal, Chhattisgarh, Madhya Pradesh, girls education has been encouraged through various schemes like provision of bicycles, mobile phones for girl students at secondary school level. Due to these efforts and modern thinking within the tribal society, the rate of girl education has increased more than before.

Politics:

Political participation is particularly effective for women's empowerment. Constituent participation is one of the ways to ensure women's empowerment through increased decision-making and greater empowerment. Women are not given due importance and credit at government level. Women's dominance is not confined to the family or social or political spheres. It is to be noted that every gram panchayat has one woman member. But women are never seen attending panchayat meetings or actively participating in panchayat proceedings. This shows that women have very little importance in decision making in tribal communities. Women are usually sidelined because they lack the necessary skills and participate in women's domestic responsibilities at home, which makes decision-making difficult. As a result men take up more profitable activities. This scenario is seen in all patriarchal and matriarchal tribal groups.

Employment:

Traditionally once upon a time tribals used to earn their livelihood by hunting and gathering forest resources. But after the Forest Conservation Act was enacted from 1952, they ran into trouble. It was a question of fate for them to provide meager food. Most of the tribals are landless. Both men and women who own land work on their land. But women were barred from plowing. Those who do not have land work as laborers on other people's land. Adivasis usually do the work of harvesting and sowing seeds. A large number of tribal women are found working in coal mines and factories. Tribal women work as tea workers in the tea plantations of North Bengal. Nowadays, many tribal girls are seen working in courts, hospitals and educational institutions in urban areas.

But most of the tribal women are engaged in household work. Those whose families had no income earners like widows used to go to the market to sell various kinds of goods. Rearing of ducks, chickens, pigs, goats and cattle has always been the exclusive sphere of economic earning of tribal women. They were even very skilled in some handicrafts useful for daily use, such as for domestic use they could make beautiful mats out of bamboo baskets, petaris (baskets with lids), benas (hand fans), grass and palm and palm leaves. They were able to support the family by making these items and selling them in the market. But with the change in the present era, they are involved in different jobs as per their qualifications and needs. They have built a pig farm, chicken farm, goat farm for income which gives them a lot of money. After getting ST Certificate they work as Group D, Railway workers, Clerks in different schools and even teachers.

Conclusion:

Change is a natural as well as a social process. So the life of tribal women cannot be an exception. Scheduled Tribes including women need to take various developmental programs by providing welfare projects and programs. Adivasi women are economically backward, so there is a need for serious efforts by the government to help improve the standard of living. Proper implementation of education has enabled rural tribal women to overcome traditional prejudices and prejudices, caste, class, gender, occupation and social barriers to live with dignity and self-reliance. Despite various constitutional provisions and policies for tribals, it is a fact that tribal women still lag behind in many areas. The government is providing a lot of support and grants for the education of tribal students, which will help increase the literacy rate and lead it in the right direction of development. Thus increasing the literacy rate and providing gainful employment opportunities for tribal women will help to change the status of tribal women in India and successfully manage the challenges.

CHAPTER TEN

INDIAN CONSTITUTION AND TRIBES

Introduction

One of the greatest political documents in the world, the Indian Constitution provides identification to over a billion people. The Indian Constitution was enacted on January 26, 1950, and has subsequently undergone a number of modifications. Indians had a sense of national maturity that permitted a rational approach to the formation and operation of government as a result of their professional accomplishments in the arts and sciences of the modern world, their pride in their rich cultural heritage, and their belief in their capacity to govern themselves. One of the oldest and most complex systems of group preference may be found in India, where the political system is mostly committed to liberal democratic ideals. On December 9, 1946, the Constituent Assembly convened as planned, with the Muslim League abstaining from its meetings. In the assembly's deliberations, the issue of minorities was seen as encompassing the claims of three different types of communities: religious minorities, backward castes, and tribal, for each of which the British and Princely States had established safeguards in various forms during the colonial era. The most outspoken tribal representative during this time refused to refer to tribes as "minorities," yet insisting that his group was entitled to special considerations. On numerous aspects, tribal claims paralleled those of the Scheduled Castes. Both factions would send forth representatives who would claim to be the original occupants of the area, making their claims preceding all others. Tribes in India, as in other parts of the world, are known for their distinctive cultures and distinctive ways of life, which give them a unique identity on the national stage. However, their odd way of life, rudimentary technologies, and propensity to live in remote places have made them economically poor, underdeveloped, and separated from the rest of the country. In order to better the socioeconomic situations of these communities, known as Scheduled Tribes, special governmental initiatives were implemented after Independence (especially following the promulgation of the Constitution of India in 1950). The tribal areas have a significant amount of racial and environmental variety. Tribal communities vary in terms of their socioeconomic standing, degree of education, and cultural context. Due to historical factors, these groups have continued to be socially, economically, and educationally disadvantaged. Since the start of the planning era, concerted efforts have been made to improve these groups' circumstances and advance their social, economic, and educational standing.

The policymakers, administrators, and social scientists in India have been perplexed by the issue of tribal development for a long time since it is urgently needed to address the issues of famine, malnutrition, inadequate housing, and exploitation that practically all trial groups in this nation experience. Before India gained its independence, the British colonial rulers isolated tribes under the adage "leave them alone," which benefited vested interests like landowners and zamindars. To steal and exploit the tribal lands and forests, which were the foundation of their economy, by hiring loggers and moneylenders. The tribal economy collapsed as a result of this policy of "neglect coupled by encroachers on the tribal's rights in land and forest," leaving them in complete poverty and misery.

Bharatratna Dr. Babasaheb Ambedkar and the other founding fathers of the constitution were aware of the political, social, and economic inequities that still existed in the nation today as a result of historical factors. They were aware of the current deplorable and horrific situations that the scheduled Tribes, who had been left behind and excluded from national life, were experiencing. In order to equalize those who were too weak to compete with the advanced segment of society in the race of life, it became necessary to implement a policy of protective discrimination. The President has the authority under the constitution to designate any territory as a scheduled area. The president may change its boundaries or enhance or decrease its area. After speaking with the governor, he may withdraw the designation, or he may issue new orders redefining the scheduling areas. The executive power of the state extends to the regions therein that are scheduled, subject to the terms of this schedule. Each year, or whenever the President so requests, the governor of each state with scheduled areas submits a report to the president on the state's management of its scheduled regions. The union has the authority to guide the state on how to manage these areas as part of its executive authority.

Even though the fifth and sixth schedules of the Indian Constitution grant scheduled tribes special status, their general situation, particularly in terms of their health, is still not good. The provision in Article 339 that the President shall appoint a Commission to report on the administration of what are known as the Scheduled Areas (i.e., areas with a preponderance of tribal population) and the welfare of the Scheduled Tribes serves as an example of the Indian Constitution's concern for the tribal population.

Tribal Courts

The Indian Reorganization Act of 1934 is responsible for the majority of current tribal courts. Prior to the Act, tribal judicial systems were built around the federal Office of Indian Affairs' Courts of Indian Offenses, which were founded in the 1880s. After the Indian Reorganization Act was passed, the tribes were able to build up their own governments, with their own courts, constitutions, and laws through tribal councils. A comprehensive history of Indian tribal autonomy under the US Constitution is given in Broken Landscape.

- One of America's foremost experts on Indian tribal law, Frank Pommersheim, presents a fresh and thoroughly studied synthesis of this legal history from the colonial period to the present, facing the shortcomings of constitutional analysis in modern Indian law jurisprudence. He shows how the federal government has consistently disregarded the recognition of tribal sovereignty in the Constitution. Instead, in its interactions with tribes, it has encouraged excessive, unchecked control. Broken Landscape encourages us to give Native American tribes and individuals the respect and decency they deserve. In the web of Indian law theory and practice, tribal courts have risen to prominence.

- This prominence is largely attributable to tribal courts' growing significance in Indian country as a source of justice and fair play, a custodian of tribal culture, and a touchstone of tribal sovereignty. This newly discovered ascendancy has also prompted important and intriguing concerns regarding the relationship between tribal courts and federal courts, both practically and legally. Despite these significant changes, little is known about the origins and growth of tribal courts

outside of the exclusive realm of Indian law academia and practice.
- This is regrettable. The problems that tribal courts must deal with have enormous implications for not simply what takes place in Indian nation and on reservations, but also for the purpose and integrity of the dominant judicial system and for society at large. Basically, we need to add a grounded thread to our existing webs of fundamental legal concepts.

Rights Of Tribal

There are numerous tribes all throughout the world, yet despite the attention paid to their distinctive customs, their rights are sometimes disregarded. By emphasizing food security, health, education, employment, and income production, development planning in India has aimed to nurture their social and economic empowerment. It is completely improper for anthropologists to view a tribe as a small, culturally distinct, economically self-sufficient society with a unique language and a self-governing political structure. Smaller, isolated, technologically dated cultures have either vanished off the face of the earth or have merged with one of the world's bigger civilizations.

Indian law typically bends in from an off direction when it connects with a wider body of jurisprudence. One result is that legal rules at play in Indian country typically vary from American law as it operates generally. Thus, special principles apply within Indian reservations in many fields of law, including criminal and civil jurisdiction, tort and contract law, and even constitutional law.

The Indian Civil Rights Act of 19681 provided a legislative answer to the question of whether, and to what extent, fundamental civil liberties recognized in constitutional law should constrain federally recognized Indian Tribes2 in the exercise of their sovereign powers.

India participated in the voting for the United Nations Declaration on the Rights of Indigenous People (UNDRIP), which was adopted in 2007. The UNDRIP recognizes, among other things, the rights of indigenous peoples to self-determination, autonomy, or self-governance, as well as their right against being forcibly ejected from or relocated to their lands or territories without their free, prior, and informed consent.

The International Labor Organization (ILO) Convention concerning Indigenous and Tribal Peoples, 1989, which is based on "respect for the cultures and ways of life of indigenous peoples" and recognizes their "right to land and natural resources and to define their own priorities for development," is another option in addition to the UNDRIP. Domestically, the Fifth and Sixth Schedules of the Constitution grant autonomy to tribal areas in terms of governance. This is further strengthened by the Samatha v. State of Andhra Pradesh & Ors. Decision of the Supreme Court from 1997, which ruled that the transfer of tribal land to private parties for mining was illegal under the Fifth Schedule. The Recognition of Forest Rights Act, 2006, which safeguards tribal people's individual and collective rights in forest areas as well as their right to give their free and informed consent in the event of their displacement and resettlement, further strengthens the framework for the protection of their rights.

Status Of Tribal Women

All people are free and entitled to the same rights at birth. But men and women are in chains everywhere. Women are generally underpowered in developing nations like India, and tribal women in particular lack access to resources and decision-making authority. Everyone has the right to live their life as a human. Human rights are neither granted nor endowed. They've already integrated themselves into society. Human rights are the preservation of fundamental freedoms including life, liberty, and property. These rights are available to everyone, irrespective of social class, caste, gender, ethnicity, or religion. The central and state governments in India have the authority to put an end to violations of human rights thanks to the constitution's preamble.

Tribal women frequently and flagrantly have their human rights violated. About 8% of all Indians are considered tribal, and these poor women live in material conditions that include low income, subpar nutrition, and limited access to health care, education, and training. The urgent need is to "empower" tribal women so that they can live lives of equality and dignity, which our society denies them. There are numerous legal measures expressly for defending the rights of tribal women, which demonstrates India's commitment to protecting its tribal community at the national level.

The most vulnerable and underprivileged population in India has historically been tribal women, who experience numerous forms of social exclusion, gender discrimination, exploitation, violence, and abuse. The Indian government has made a number of promises, especially for tribal members, and is making a lot of effort to provide them the same standing as other citizens.

Although there are legal protections in place to protect tribal women from marginalization, Indian culture does not succeed in achieving these goals of equality and social justice.

CHAPTER ELEVEN

THE EFFECTS OF SOCIAL MEDIA ON INDIAN TRIBAL CULTURE

Introduction

The media today has well and truly spread its wings. The use of social media has drawn significant role in recent years. An increasing number of practitioners have started using social media in their teaching. From being limited to the whims of a few individuals, it has come a long way to become a means of social participation. While the fourth estate has been in order for a long while, it seems to have realized its true potential and purpose in the new millennium only in the true spirit of democracy as envisaged by Abraham Lincoln's of being an institution 'of the people, by the people and for the people'. This has been facilitated by the advent of the social media. Social media, with its immediate and amplified reach, has transformed the way people interact with each other. This is significant because information and social awareness have emerged as important factors of human empowerment. The focus of this paper is to delineate the relationship between social media and Tribal India. This paper is an attempt at 'connecting media with society' as it relates to the problems being faced by the tribal people in the predominantly tribal and rural district in India. The theoretical framework for this study thus includes, (i) Media Theories of Communication, and (ii) the Sociological models of Social Change. The objective in this paper is to examine the role of television as a medium for social upliftment. The efficacy of television is assessed as to how far it is effective in disseminating information about the potential benefits of the existing schemes aimed at tribal development.

Impact of Social Media:-

The Indian society is an elaborate society with multi cultures, multi tribes and castes, multi lingual and the disparities between the urban and rural people. Since the birth of independent India, there is no denying the fact that India has grown as a nation and as economy rapidly with major growths from infrastructure to public health care, from communication sector to IT field and much more. But development is not a linear process but a multifaceted system with a complex idea. Even the rural India defies any definition of development. The Indian government has started many initiatives which have tried to encompass the large Indian crowd and while also many UN programs have been put to use in Indian villages. Besides that, many private social networks have taken the initiative like various NGOs, news channels, various web sites etc. But unlike Europe's systematic Industrial growth, Asia and Africa still remain largely unaffected by the model due to the large size of many nations with no connectivity. India goes through a similar problem. That's the reason when rural areas of India still face issues like sanitation, public health care etc., social media finds a relevant place. Diverse social and infrastructural needs must be addressed more or less simultaneously to ensure a nation's future growth and prosperity. Social media has affected all spheres of rural people's lives: right from their livelihood to their healthcare, from traditions to social campaigns etc. Time and time again SNS have found a way and have realized their potential to become pioneers in rural development. Many Indian social media networks have committed themselves to provide information to the farmers regarding cultivation as well as animal husbandry especially All India Radio (AIR) which has been committed to rural audience for more than 50 years now.

Among the several mass media, newspaper and farm magazine are commonly used. They have a vital role to play in the communication of agricultural information among the literate farmers. Increasing rate of literacy in the country offers new promises and prospects for utilizing print medium as a means of mass communication. Agriculture journalism is a new field in India and is growing rapidly as the food giver of India is becoming literate now (Rai & Shahila, 2013). Through online public grievance system, development in these parts take place smoothly as the villagers can lodge their complaints on this forum. This initiative has aided rural people a lot. Though it is naive to think that electricity, telephony and connectivity in rural areas will spread if the demand does not grow of these resources.

In addition, information networks can become conduits that allow money to flow into the village through new kinds of non-discriminatory and clean industries. Information and communications technologies can also compensate for other kinds of infrastructure limitations. For example, if online work, trade, or payment were to become available for members of a village community, the poor quality of roads to and from that village becomes less of an obstacle to earnings and employment. Finally, and most importantly, if capital were to become more readily available within a village community through such networked systems, it would then be in a better position to finance the basic infrastructure that it needs, including roads, dispensaries, and water and sanitation systems. (Rai & Shahila, 2013) But there has been a critical problem, the problem has been of digital divide. The global digital divide describes the unequal distribution of information and communication technology across nations, commonly described as the "gap between the information haves and have-nots." The contours of the global digital divide are complex and, although the "digital divide" has become a common political catchphrase, popular discourse has, for the most part, failed to capture all of the dimensions of the divide. (Ali, 2011) The Internet has transfigured the way most people in the West live. It has become an important part of our economic, political, and social lives, changing the way we purchase commodities, the way we bank, and the way we share exchanges with one another. First, the Internet reduces traditional blockages to trade and industry, allowing small businesses in developing nations to market their products directly to the United States and other developed countries. Second, the informational capacity of the Internet enabled developing countries to move ahead in improving fundamental services. It can allow, with its use, people all across to access information from any part of the world. The only way in India to reduce this divide is by providing the rural people with adequate information on the internet and its uses explained. But there would be people on the internet looking to cash in for the naïve nature of new internet users. But amongst many limitations, digital divide is said to be only temporary as technology would become redundant in developed nations and the third world countries would be able to produce this technology for cheaper rates, they would also be able to improve their existing technology. These gaps in connectivity is due to the economic disparity of different nations, whereas some nations have tried to improve this connectivity but there are many pressing issues in third world countries, for instance, irregular electricity supply. The problem then lies with the fact that rural India needs platforms where they could express their grievances, like, online public grievance. Social media can provide this platform where their voices and their culture is protected, looked after.In today's global economy, where computers and the Internet are so fundamental to production and participation, it is clear that if the right to development is to be taken seriously, that right must encompass the development of information connectivity technology infrastructure and skills. It is also very important to look at the various platforms which have helped rural India, where there was definite impact made on the lives of the people. These are just examples to clarify the impact.

History of Social Media:-

Social media is intelligent, connectedness, and client produced content. At present the utilization of web-based media has become an essential day by day action. The primary informal organization site, SixDegrees.com, was dispatched in 1997. In India, Orkut beat among the long range informal communication sites with a client portion of 64% (Madhavan, 2007). In the article of Complete history on social media highlighted (Hendrick, 8th May 2013), primary conspicuous web-based media website, Six Degrees, was made in 1997. In 1999, the first contributing to a blog locales got mainstream, making an online media impression that is as yet well known today. After the appearance of writing for a blog, openness of online media extraordinarily upgraded. Locales like My Space and LinkedIn acquired noticeable quality in the mid-2000s, and destinations like Photobucket and Flickr worked with online photograph sharing. Revelation of YouTube occurred in the year 2005, making an altogether new path for individuals to impart and impart to one another across huge spans. By 2006, other two more conspicuous online media ran over Facebook and Twitter both opened up to clients all through the world [1]. So from the above confirmations it very well may be hypothesize that the fate of interpersonal interaction may glance in the following decade or even 100 years from now, and it tends to be anticipated that the bedrock of web-based media will be at top as the long as the existence person is supported in the earth.

The significance of the study: -

• As Television has an important role as an agent of social change aimed at social upliftment in dissemination of information, spread of education, the tribal people in remote areas can use it, for their benefit.

• As a companion, Television can provide through step by step identification, description, discussion, and

solutions of the issues being faced by tribal people.

• Participation and involvement of tribal people in special audience program is the key to ensure development.

• Developmental issues of tribal people are addressed by the Television like other issues such as displacement, migration, unemployment, deforestation.

• Television programmes focuses on the success stories of tribal people for others to emulate.

• A Special supplements which caters to the needs of tribal people and give sufficient space to the cases of female feticide.

• Knowledge about vocational course related to tribal people is imparted, which helps in getting vocational jobs or helps in self-employment.

Television disseminates information on a mass scale, which ensures that every tribal area will be heard in their hour of need and ensure safety and justice to tribal people, which will also enhance their personality. The Television will broadcast the Tribal people's opinion when policies and schemes are being implanted, which will provide a monitoring,evaluation and feedback to the administrators. The television thus can serve as an agent of social change aimed at social upliftment in disseminating technical knowhow on the one hand, and will help reduce inequalities in socio-economic opportunities as the broadcasting at the mass level will aid literacy, health, population control by motivation a desire for change and mobility among the not so aware of the opportunities made available by Government schemes and projects.

Problems being faced by the tribal people:-

While substantial amount of studies on tribal population are available, but not many systematic, methodological

and empirical studies as such are available, most of whom dwell in far flung inaccessible rural areas, when various tribes in the predominantly tribal district differ so much in their rituals and daily chores of life.

In view of the above problems being faced by tribal people, the following are the significant issues of the Study:

1. High level of illiteracy in itself, and very low when compared with their male counterparts, literacy from a mere 4%, a giant leap forward, but still at 23%, a long, long way to go,

2. Early marriage reduces chances of education, thereby reducing or delaying their contribution in the sustenance of economy, i.e. social change aimed at social upliftment , decreasing their sources of earning livelihood on their own,

3. Tribal people remain engaged in superstitious, Rituals, traditional beliefs, thereby developing a culture centric mechanism,

4. Lot of work, forest, cooking woods picking, and animal grazing: gathering products from the forest areas, working in agriculture, substantially involved in household and domestic activities, collection of fire wood, drinking water, care of children and cooking, and so and so forth,

5. Cultural heritage like tribal women wearing decorative beads, heavily laden nose, ear and ankle rings, throat rings, to turn the women folks at times like an adorable piece of art, rather than a human being contributing in the process of social change aimed at social upliftment. While the traits of rich cultural heritage of the tribal women must be protected and preserved at all costs, but at the same time it should not come as an hindrance in the larger process of social change aimed at social upliftment.

6. Women become intended, or unintended, victim of male chauvinism in a traditional society, where anxiety and restrictions on their freedom and dignity remain a built-in social mechanism, causing their subjugation and marginalization.

7. The institutional process of development carried from outside forces like Gov't in the name of development and modernization, i.e. a top-down approach rather than building from bottom-up, has also been a cause of concern to the freedom and independence of tribal, which at times is being perceived as unduly imposed and interfering in their natural way of life living in harmony and proximity with jal, jangal, jamin and janwar (water, forest, land, and animals)

8. The process of development involving mega projects of international dimensions through multinational corporations like building dams, large scale mining, deforestation, special economic zones causing deforestation, all are uprooting tribal population,

Conclusion:-

Without a doubt changed the lives of tribal people. As far as agriculture is thought of, these have given many opportunities to the farmers and made the process of selling the crop easy through online programs which have resulted in the removal of middlemen. There are many success stories in field of health care as well. Rural politics is the area where social media network's hasn't reached to the required potential. But there still remains a lot of room for improvement for social networking services as with better technology, the connectivity of these places should improve and provide the economic opportunity to take benefits from the system. Social Media can help provide that, media which cares for a well-integrated society and believes in having social responsibility.

Services like Face book, twitter provide a mass reach, but of a population which can afford to have the required technology to avail the service but can help connect the large population. The requirement is of the necessary technology from which these platforms can be accessed. Once accessed, it is important that social media doesn't influence the people in a way that alienates them from the real potential of these platforms. The impact can be seen through many examples and these examples are of not just Social media like – Face book but with the use of internet NGO's like Gramvaani have flourished, defining social media in a new perspective which is of development and of a social responsibility.

CHAPTER TWELVE

TRIBAL SOCIO-ECONOMIC, CULTURAL, AND EDUCATION PROBLEMS

Introduction:

India is a country full of biodiversity where people of different cultures live. Tribes are the people with different way of living and community Life. Tribes are people of different lifestyles. They live in certain geographical areas across 18 percent of the country. According to the 2011 census, the indigenous people constitute 8.6 per cent of the country's 104 million population. Their own culture, customs, religious beliefs, etc. are quite different from other tribal communities. In general, Scheduled Tribes are far behind economically, socio-culturally and educationally, so their problems are different from other communities. Indigenous literacy is much lower than that of the general population. Analysis of various environmental indicators and their meanings on social and cultural educational status shows why special attention needs to be paid to them. Generally far behind the citizens. 58% of the indigenous community lives below the poverty line. The saddest thing is that 52% of the tribal are deprived of transport and communication facilities.

OBJECTIVE OF THE STUDY

The main objectives of the study are

- To study the historical background of Tribal community.
- To find out Issues that impact on Tribal education.
- To identify some critical issues and challenges of Tribal development.
- To understand the importance of education in tribal development.

Types of Tribes:

West Bengal, Mizoram, Nagaland, Andhra Pradesh, Madhya Pradesh and Bihar, Assam having maximum number of tribal communities. But Madhya Pradesh is the largest state of the country in terms of tribal population. Accordingto the 20011 census, includes 1 crore 53 lakh 16 thousand 784 population of Madhya Pradesh. Some important tribal groups are:

- Jarawa in Andaman
- Bhot in Himachal Pradesh
- Bhil also found in Rajasthan, some in Gujarat and Maharashtra
- Ao in Nagaland
- Jaintia in Meghalaya
- Kuki in Manipur
- karkari in Madhya Pradesh
- Mundas tribe is found in Bihar, orrisha, west Bengal.
- purnia in Bihar.
- Todas in nilgiriand Irula in Tamil Nadu.
- Warlis in Maharashtra
- Angami in Monipur
- Tripuri in Tripura
- Bodo in Assam
- Rabha in Assam

Nature of Tribal:

A tribe is a territorial community. These families which normally have blood relationships among themselves could be matriarchal or patriarchal in nature.

Every tribe has its own name. Each tribe is known to other tribes by its distinctive name. Example of some Indian tribes: Garo, Khasi, Mandi, orao, Majhi, Santhal, Naga Limbu, Sema Naga, Khasa. The daily life of the indigenous community is full of challenges. They face various social problems for their survival. Indigenous people live as forced laborers. Even at the lowest levels of society Works. Tribal communities like Dom, Chamar and Kultar serve all upper caste families. Examples of limitations are the Sagari system in Rajasthan, the Veti system in Andhra Pradesh, the Gothi system in Orissa, the Jetha system in Karnataka and the boat service in Chhattisgarh. They borrowed money from moneylenders, but could not pay, so they were forced to work until the loan was repaid. In India, tribal communities are the least educated. First generation students have to face social, emotional and cultural barriers to get an education. Another reason is the poor performance of Indigenous students in schools. They are deprived of nutritious food. Most of the tribal people in India are illiterate. Tribes find the existence of deities in trees, animals, rocks, wood etc. They believe in the old method and also rely on local herbal medicines. In most cases, the tribes marry into their own group. Indigenous literacy, education rates, health, malnutrition and economic conditions hinder progress.

MAJOR ISSUE AND PROBLEMS OF TRIBES:

Social problem: The biggest problem of the tribes is the social problem. Tribes from the past to the present they live with their ritual principles such as animal sacrifice, black magic, child marriage, and wife change all these cultures. Moreover, they believe in the worship of family deities, the worship of nature, and symbols and even socio-political institutions are dependent on religious institutions.

Cultural problem: The culture of the tribes is one of the most important aspects of development. The cultural features of tribal societies are that they are quite different from other social cultures. Each indigenous group has its own cultural environment. Conduct of tribal society Behavior, customs, way of life, customs, and culture are different from other educated, civilized society.

Poverty: The majority of the tribes live below the poverty line. Most of the tribes have chosen hunting, fish farming, beggar work, brick kiln work and agriculture as their primary occupations. In such an economy there is no profit and no surplus. So the per capita income there is very low compared to the average Indian income. Most of them live below the poverty line and are in debt to local moneylenders and zamindars. They often mortgage their land or sell it to moneylenders to pay off debts. Debt is almost inevitable because these moneylenders have to pay heavy interest. Banking facilities in tribal areas are so inadequate that tribal's are forced to rely on moneylender.

Nutrition problem: There are vast differences in the health status of mothers and children between tribal and non-tribal populations. A significant obstacle to the provision of public health services to the tribal population is the reluctance to hire trained doctors, nurses, technicians, managers and healthcare workers in designated areas. Medical insurance coverage like health insurance scheme (RSBY) is very low in designated areas. That is why the people of the Scheduled Tribes are living a sick life.

Infant mortality rates have been found to be very high in some tribes due to malnutrition. But in 2021, the infant mortality rate in India was 28.771 deaths per 1000 live births. In many parts of India, tribal peoples suffer from chronic infections, waterborne diseases, scarcity, and the Himalayan tribes suffer from common diseases such as leprosy and tuberculosis due to iodine deficiency.

Drinking water problem: The biggest problem of tribal society is lack of drinking water. The inaccessible roads, scattered houses, and lack of roads to the inner villages have hampered the safe drinking water supply in the tribal areas. Many tribal homes do not have clean water. As a result, tribal people often get sick from drinking contaminated water from T-storms and springs. And children have to face diseases like tuberculosis, cholera, typhoid etc. Women have to walk a long way to get clean drinking water.

Education Problem: Illiteracy is the biggest problem of tribal society. Education has had little effect on tribal groups. There was no direct government program for their education before. But in the following years, some changes have been made in the reservation policy. Yet at present the illiteracy rate in tribal society is 70%. Yet they are trapped in a web of linguistic problems and prejudices. They are still far from the boundaries of modern education. Indigenous people live in a dark world. It is not easy for most tribes living in extreme poverty to send their children to school. Since most of the tribes live in the western and remote areas, the indifference of the teachers can be noticed.

Unemployment: Unemployment is another problem in tribal society. Since the tribes live in forest and hilly areas. So they do not have any specific industry and job opportunities. So the tribes are unemployed. They make a living from sources of income such as basket weaving, weaving, fish farming, hunting, animal husbandry, poultry, agriculture and handicrafts.

Communication problem: Communication is an important issue for tribal communities. Since the language of the tribal community is very different from other communities, the tribal children do not understand the official or regional language used by the teacher in the classroom. They only understand their mother tongue. Since there are no tribal teachers in tribal schools in India, non-tribal teachers are recruited. So the teacher does not understand the language of the children and vice versa the students also do not understand the language of the teachers. Lack of trained teachers Due to shortage of teachers, tribal schools cannot attract students and create interest in teaching tribal students. In some cases, tribal teachers are not educated in higher education and their educational qualifications are below tenth grade, which adversely affects the education of students.

Transport problem: Most of the tribal areas are hilly. Lack of proper paved roads, fear of wild animals, inconvenience of transportation system and lack of electric lighting in the roads, children and tribal people have to face various problems. They have to walk a long way to school and market.

MAJOR PROBLEMS TO SOLVE THE SOCIAL, ECONOMIC AND EDUCATIONAL PROBLEM:

The main challenges in solving social, economical and educational problems:

1. Superstition Reform Fence: Indigenous people are still living in the darkness of ignorance. This modern society is so advanced yet they believe in their customs, rituals, superstitions, black magic, and herbal medicine.

2. Social inequality: Tribal community culture is very different from other community culture. They cannot adapt to other community cultures. As a result, social inequality can be noticed.

3. Untouchability: The position of the lowest level tribes in the hierarchical class of human society. They are an exploited and deprived and neglected community. Civilized society deprives them of all aspects so this nation is commonly known as untouchability.

4. Reluctance to go to school: Most of the parents of tribal children are not educated enough. It goes without saying that they have no general knowledge about education. They do not know the value of education so they cannot create interest in sending their child to school.

5. Economic burden: Sources of income in tribal areas are agriculture, bricklaying, fish farming, poultry farming. Indigenous people are indebted to moneylenders in various ways. So parents involve their children in work to reduce the economic burden.

6. Teacher indifference towards tribal children: As most of the teachers are from other languages, the children of the community are not properly educated. And since children in tribal communities do not know any language other than their mother tongue, the teacher often scolds, insults and physically punishes the child, so the child leaves school for fear of the teachers. And the teachers look at the children of the tribal community differently from the children of other nations. As a result, tribal children are reluctant to come to school.

7. Child marriage: Child marriage is a big problem in every society. Parents of tribal families do not support their children to continue their education. Especially in the case of girl child. After marriage, a girl is bound by social responsibilities and household chores.

8. Narrow mindedness: In tribal society, boys and girls are treated differently. The mentality of the parents of a girl child is bound by the old rules, laws, discipline. They think that the girl will be married one day or the other so they do not need to be educated in higher education. They should do the housework which is enough for them.

9. Corruption: The Central and State Governments have arranged various projects for the SC, ST community such as scholarships, free admission, free uniforms, free books, lunch, bags, stationery, bicycles, phones, Etc. These benefits do not reach the concerned tribal community due to corruption.

Conclusion: From the above discussion, it is clear that the indigenous people need to be fully developed and deep initiatives need to be taken for the betterment of the tribal community. Poverty, economy, malnutrition, their housing, debt, unemployment, loss of natural resources, inadequate transportation facilities, inadequate education facilities, poor medical facilities, social exclusion, educational problems and inequality etc. They face a daily challenge. In order to overcome all these problems, they need to be socially conscious and educated. Moreover, as they live in hilly areas or forests, they are deprived of proper transport and communication system. But they cannot enroll their children in school due to economic weakness. Lack of trained teachers in tribal areas, language problems, communication problems, tribal education are also major obstacles to social development.

The government has implemented various projects and programs for the formulation and implementation of tribal sub-plans for the socio-economic development of the tribes such as scholarships, free uniforms, book banks in primary schools, road development, adult education activities, universal education campaign, improvement of English education in tribal areas, mid-day meal. Something like planned. Has made serious efforts for development in tribal areas but there are some big challenges to solve the above problems. Most of the time tribal parents are reluctant to send their children to school. Abuse of teachers, child marriage, superstition, deprivation of all government facilities, narrow mindedness of parents towards education. Thus we have discussed various aspects of tribal communities; the main problems and challenges they face. We can improve their quality of life by inspiring them and providing incentives for educational setups. Tribes are an integral part of the Indian population and play an important role in enriching Indian culture. Today the tribal community is much more advanced than in the past.

CHAPTER THIRTEEN

INDIAN TRIBAL MOVEMENT

Introduction

Tribal community is one of the oldest and main indigenous people of India. It is believed that they are the real owners of the land from the beginning of civilization in India till today. From time immemorial, they have been referred to as tribals. "Indigenous" which means the homeland of the old civilization. Over time, the wheel of civilization began to roll and the light of civilization reached day by day. But this tribal community seems to be a little behind other tribes and they remain out of the mainstream. However, at present, various initiatives have been taken to improve them and bring light to the way of life. The most well-known of these tribes are Bhil, Munda, Santal, Orao etc. Mainly due to their aggressive attitude towards the British in the contemporary situation, they have taken place in the pages of history as a chapter in a bright light and as a struggling tribe.

Outbursts of tribal resentment: From the last period of Mughal rule, colonial rule flourished in India. When the Permanent Settlement introduced by Lord Cornwallis came into force in 1793 and various forms of introduction were introduced, resistance and rebellion against the British rule began to appear. Tribal communities They lived independently at the foot of the mountains, in the open space in the forest. But when the British powers imposed extra taxes on those places day after day and took over their rights and started oppressing the tribes to collect taxes, the tribal community revolted against the British and eventually took the form of a tribal rebellion. The tribal movements against the British rule in different parts of India began to grow day by day.

Pahariyas Rebellion: The Pa hariyas were a tribal group in Santal Pargana's Rajmahal Hills. Prior to the arrival of British rule in India, they had maintained virtual independence.These people regarded the entire territory to be their country, and they were hostile to strangers. Because of their geographical seclusion, the Paharias had always preserved their independence prior to the arrival of the British.Due to their means of existence being insufficient, especially during times of famine, the Paharias frequently plundered the plains held by settled agriculturists.These invasions also served as a means of demonstrating dominance over the established settlements.The lowlands zamindars customarily paid a regular tribute to the Paharias to buy peace, much as traders paid the hill leaders to utilize the passages controlled by them.This fairly brittle peace agreement, however, dissolved in the late eighteenth century as established agriculture grew in eastern India, with the British pushing forest removal.

The expansion of established agriculture reduced the area of underwoods and pastures, causing friction between hill inhabitants and settled cultivators.The Pahariyas began raiding established settlements more often. In the 1770s, the British launched a merciless campaign against the Pahariyas, hunting them out and murdering them.The Pahariyas revolt of 1778, led by Raja Jagganath, is noteworthy.In the 1780s, the British instituted a pacification strategy, in which Paharia leaders were granted an annual allowance in exchange for ensuring that their troops behaved correctly.This policy was not accepted by all Pahariyas. Some of them retreated deep into the mountains, away from enemy troops, to continue the struggle against the diku, or 'outsiders.'

Kol Rebellion: (1831) Cole Rebellion is one of the most important tribal revolts. The tribals of Chhotanagpur region were divided into different communities like Ho, Munda, Orao etc. They lived independently in this area. In 1820, the king of Porhat surrendered to the British and agreed to pay a large annual tax and claimed the surrounding area as his own. The British government finally accepted it. There was a great dissatisfaction among the Coles when it came to collecting rent from this region. The Coles even rebelled and killed the royal officials. In this situation, a group of soldiers led by a general named Rogses came to the aid of the king of Porhat. With bows and arrows and spears, Colera fought to the death against the English and forced the defeated army to retreat. The following year, in 1821, despite strong resistance against the British, the forest children were defeated by British cannons and forced to surrender.

A decade later, in 1831, the kol rebelled. The Chhotanagpur area was leased to Hindu-Muslim and Sikh moneylenders for revenue collection. The British workers started brutally torturing the Coles to collect the revenue and take away all their belongings. In addition, the judiciary and the law hurt the ancient social system. Eventually, in protest of so much oppression, exploitation and harassment, Buddha Bhagat, Zoya Bhagat, Jhindrai Manik and Sui Munda started gathering. In 1831, the farmers of Munda, Orao community of Ranchi district declared the first revolt. The news gradually spread to Singbhum, Manbhum, Hazaribagh, Palamau districts. The rebels resorted to unlimited cruelty and the zamindars, moneylenders, English workers and even non-indigenous people were not spared. Because they considered zamindars, traders and moneylenders as part of the English rule. The rebels set fire to the houses of moneylenders, zamindars and traders and brutally killed them. Only blacksmiths and carpenters escaped their attack. Because they needed to make weapons and other goods. The army came from Danapur and Patna to suppress the rebellion. The army clashed with the rebels in different places. Two years later, the British forces used modern weapons against the bow and arrow and finally won. Thousands of tribes brutally killed men, women and children and suppressed the revolt in 1833. The end of this tribal movement is marked in Indian history.

Chuar Rebellion: The Chuar Rebellion was one of the most important tribal revolts. They were usually a primitive tribe of Chuars. They lived in Jangalmahal of Bankura and parts of Medinipur district. They made their living mainly by farming and hunting animals. But the zamindars and moneylenders forced the British to revolt if they exceeded the limits of tax collection. The Chua Rebellion began in 1766-1772 and lasted until 1795-1816. They led the revolt mainly from Manbhum and Barabhum. The revolt was most intense, especially between Ghatshila and Barabhum hills. They also changed their lands from time to time and focused on hunting. But in 1784 Jagannath Singh, the zamindar of Ghatshila, adopted a strict policy against the Chuars and in 1771, with the help of the company, suppressed about 1000 Chuars and occupied the whole area. Under these circumstances, Chuar Sardar Dadkar Shyamganj, Subala Singh of Kalipal, and Dubraj declared rebellion against the zamindars. However, the rebellion was suppressed by the British government. The most important revolt of the Chuars was against Durjan Singh, the zamindar of Raipur. However, some other famous leaders of the Chuar Rebellion were Madhab Singh, the brother of the Raja of Barabhum, and Raja Mohan Singh.

Ho and Munda Rebellion: Ho and Munda Rebellion occupies a very important place when it comes to tribal rebellion. The Ho tribe of Jharkhand played an active role against various forms of oppression by the British and eventually called for rebellion. The Ho Rebellion lasted from

1827to 1837. A constructive revolt against the king of Porhat is the revolt of the Ho.

If we do not talk about the Munda Rebellion in terms of the discussion of history, a large part of the Tribal Rebellion will be left out. This Munda Rebellion is also known as "Ulgulan". The Mundas were mainly located south of Ranchi. The period of the Munda Rebellion can be traced from 1860 to 1920. However, the most powerful period is from 1899-1920. The revolt was led by Birsa Munda. The revolt against the zamindars, jagirdars, traders, contractors and moneylenders had been going on for almost thirty years.

Birsa Munda declared herself an angel of God in 1895, saying that "God has given her the miraculous power to alleviate human suffering." He is also believed to have had a vision of God. He also claims to be the "Father of the Earth." Thousands of people began to gather around him, calling him the "savior of mankind." He told his followers that God had appeared to him in a dream and told him to fight against the British. He would fight, that is, God himself would fight against us. In this way he strengthened the minds of all his followers. He started trying desperately to fight against the British. Inspired by Birsa Munder, thousands of followers jumped into the movement against the British. He even encouraged the killing of contractors, zamindars, and jagirdars, kings, magistrates, and Christians. And he said, "Satya Yuga should be established instead of the present Kali Yuga." He declared war on them. The land will be red like the red flag painted in their blood. The poor who are not indigenous should not be attacked. He raised an army of 6,000 men with bows and arrows and spears. But before the last war began, he was arrested in early February 1900 and died in prison in June. As a result, this large tribal movement seemed to disappear with the death of Birsa Munda.

Santal Rebellion: The most important history of the Tribal Rebellion discussed is the Santal Rebellion. This revolt is also known as "Hul" revolt. The Santals mainly lived in the area from Bhagalpur to Rajmahal hills. The region came under Company rule when the British government introduced the "Permanent Settlement". Under the oppression of the zamindars and the employees of the company, they left the area and cleared the forests of part of Murshidabad in the hilly region of Rajmahal and started living and farming there. They call this region "Damin-i-Koh" or "the edge of the mountains".

The Santals were generally a hardworking, peace-loving and simple agrarian indigenous community. He lived in the deep forests of Bankura, Birbhum, Medinipur, Manbhum, Chhotanagpur and Palamau areas. They were outraged when the local zamindars, the Mahajanads and the British unjustly imposed taxes on them and demanded 50 to 500 percent of the money at high interest rates. They used to call foreigners "Diku". Which means external. Dikuentangled the Santals in a debt trap in such a way that they could not repay the debt for the rest of their lives. As a result, the Santals had to lose farmland, oxen and all crops due to debt. Even the shopkeepers cheated the Santals by weighing "Kenaram" and "Becharam". In many cases, the British army and its staff would destroy the crops by leaving ponies, horses, elephants and cattle on the Santals' land. Eventually it took the form of an intense revolt known as the Santal Revolt.

The two main leaders or two brothers Sidhu and Kanu came up as the face of the protest and as the main leader. On 30th June 1855, under their leadership, about 10,000 Santals gathered in the field of Bhagana Dihi and declared the establishment of an independent Santal state. He also had two brothers named Bhairab and Bir Singh, Kalo Pramanik, Domon Majhi also led the revolt. The number of rebels began to increase day by day and reached about 50,000.

The Santals believed that God's blessing was behind their actions. The two main leaders, Sidhu and Kanu, claimed that God had met them and told them to fight for independence against the British at gunpoint. Sidhu said God appeared to me and instructed "this country is not the country of the masters but God Himself will fight against the British on their behal.

At first their activities started in the area from Bhagalpur to Munger. In different places, the Santals came together and completely cut off postal and rail communication. Railway stations, police stations and post offices were the main targets of the Europeans. The houses of the Bengali native zamindars were the target of their attack. Gradually realizing the extent of the rebellion, the government organized large-scale military operations against the rebels. Several regiments were mobilized under Major General Borough. Martial law was imposed in the rebel-held areas. The British government also announced a reward of up to Rs 10,000 if any leaders were caught.

The Santal rebellion was ruthlessly suppressed by the government. More than 15,000 Santals were killed and many villages were destroyed. By the end of 1855, there had been several battles between the rebel forces and the

British. Kalikinkar Dutt wrote, "The Santals fought valiantly, but the British, armed with modern weapons, could not succeed." By February 1855, Hul's organization was completely disbanded. The coup was suppressed by the British government. Sidhu was captured and betrayed in the midst of the mutiny, but was immediately shot dead by British forces. The whole Rajmahal hill became wet and red. And thus the revolt was ended with the death of two great leaders of Santal. Historian Ramesh Chandra Majumder writes: By 1874 the Santals had tried to regroup in some areas, but no more large-scale incidents like the Hull massacre of 1855 had taken place.

Kherwar Movement: The Kherwar Movement can be identified as part of the Santal Rebellion. This movement was a movement to return to the old tradition of the Santals. Preparation. This movement was led by Bhagirath Majhi Jadu Majhi, Piru Majhi and other prominent personalities. They started attacking government offices and zamindars' houses with their hand-made arrows, bows, clubs and other weapons. To suppress the attack, the British general Thomas Gordon suppressed the movement by ruthlessly killing many Santals with the help of 5,000 army cannons. However, in the context of this movement, the historian Suprakash Roy wrote that "this movement did not fail.

Khond Rebellion: The Khond Rebellion was an important and special rebellion in the case of tribal rebellion. The revolt was started by a tribal community in Orissa. The British government initially and later forcibly instructed the khonds to stop the "human sacrifice". This custom was a symbol of fertility in the land and a symbol of grain-greenery. The khondas, however, were the first to believe in this for a long time and their crops were also good crops. But when the British government ordered to stop it, they started a movement against the British and the revolt intensified. They started protesting against the rule of the company. Under the leadership of Raja Chakra Visnoi, the khonds started a fierce movement against the new taxes and the entry of zamindars into their area, including the cessation of human sacrifice. This movement was mainly seen in Ghumsar, Kalahandi, Patana etc. areas of Orissa.

Koya Rebellion: This revolt was seen in the East Godavari Valley of present day Andhra Pradesh. The revolt, led by khond leader Sara, began when the new British law deprived the zamindars of access to the forest. The revolts can be traced back to 1803, 1840, 1845, 1858 and 1862 AD. However, the revolt took place between 1879 and 1880 AD under the leadership of Tomma Sarah.

Bhil Rebellion: The Bhil tribe was an indigenous tribe and tribe living in the foothills of the Western Ghats. It was during this time that the Bhils started a movement against famine, financial hardship and irregular government taxes. The revolt of the Bhils was noticed in several stages in 1825, 1831 and 1848. However, the reformer Govinda Guru later helped the Bhils to unite in South Rajasthan.

Koli Rebellion: At the foot of the Western Ghats, the Koli lived as a neighbor of the Bhils. Kolis was similarly persecuted by the British Company. The Koli rebellion began with the demolition of the fort, the introduction of new laws. The Koli rebelled against the foreigners in the first phase from 1824-1839 AD and in the second phase from 1844-1848 AD.

Ramosi Rebellion: The Ramosis were also a tribal community living in the Western Ghats. They organized rebellion against the British under the leadership of Ramosi leader Chittur Singh. The movement started when the British government introduced Satara rights, integration policy, new administrative policy. Ramosis were mainly working under them during the Maratha period. But when the Maratha kingdom became part of the British Empire, the British began to influence their lives. As a result, in 1822, Chittur Singh Ramosi started a revolt. Again in 1825-26 the revolt continued till 1829 under the leadership of Umaji Naik and his supporter Bapu Trimbakji. Later, under the leadership of Raja Pratap Singh of Satara, the revolt started in 1839 and lasted till 1840-41 AD.

Tribal Rebellion in Northeast India: The arrival of the British in India and the establishment of their colonial empire all over India has been able to give a new picture to the history of India. Their dominance was established everywhere from north to south, from east to west. And in order to establish this one domination, the Indian tribes started imposing various kinds of taxes and oppression on them and the tribes. However, the Indian tribes repeatedly revolted against the establishment of British domination. Indigenous tribes were the first to play an active role in opposing the empire. The rebellion of the tribal community in Northeast India is discussed below.

Khasi Rebellion: The Khasi Rebellion was one of the most important tribal uprisings in Northeast India. The Khasi tribes generally lived between the Garo and Jayantia hills in northeastern India. However, the revolt of the Khasis began when the British East India Company began the process of building a road connecting the Brahmaputra valley to the Sylhet valley.

Because the Khasis did not see the arrival of a large number of foreign Englishmen here very well. So in protest of the construction of this road, the Khasis, Garos, Khamtis and singos, led by Tirath Singh, declared rebellion against the British. Day by day the popularity of this rebellion began to grow. But the revolt of the Khasis was suppressed in 1833 by the modern weapons of the British power. However, despite the failure, these uprisings in North-East India have occupied a significant place.

Sinfos Rebellion: The Singfos Rebellion in Assam is also one of the tribal revolts. Nirang Phidu invaded the British garrison in 1843 and led the revolt. Killed a large number of British soldiers. Many other small movements and revolts were also observed in North-East India. Has ranked as significant.

Evaluation: Therefore, we can say that although the picture of tribal revolt against the British in India started differently in different places, its main purpose was to oppose the British rule. The liberation of the British from oppression was the first time that this tribal community came out in protest of the repressive policies of the British rule which has given a new direction to the tribal movement.

References

- THE HISTORY OF TRIBAL ADMINISTRATION, https://egyankosh.ac.in/bitstream/123456789/71393/1/Unit-4.pdf
- Tribal Uprisings in the 18th and 19th Centuries, https://unacademy.com/content/mppsc/study-material/
- Tribals and Tribal Policy, https://journalsofindia.com/tribals-and-tribal-policy/, December 4, 2018
- The authors are C. von Fürer-Haimendorf and E. von Fürer-Haimendorf. (2021). The Gonds of Andhra Pradesh: Indian tribal heritage and change. Routledge.
- the following individuals: Chaubey, G., Tamang, R., Pennarun, E., Dubey, P., Rai, N., Upadhyay, R. K.,... & R. Villems (2017). Reconstructing the demographic history of the Dravidian-speaking Gond, the biggest tribe in India. 25(4), 493-498, European Journal of Human Genetics.
- B. Sinha. (2017). Life, livelihood, and educational opportunities for the Maharashtrian Katkari tribes. 6, 57–64, Indian Journal of Educational Research.
- S. C. Verma (2010). A study of sociocultural dynamics, The Eco-friendly Tharu Tribe. Asian and Pacific Studies Journal, 1 (2).
- S. C. Verma (2010). A study of sociocultural dynamics, The Eco-friendly Tharu Tribe. Asian and Pacific Studies Journal, 1 (2).
- Gordon E. Dobson (1875). about the Andaman Islands and Andamanese. Journal of the British and Irish Anthropological Institute, 4, 457-467.
- DN Purkayastha, concept of Indian tribes: an overview, Vol. 5 International Journal of Advanced Research in Management and Social Sciences.
- P Mondal, Surajit Sinha: Biography and Contribution to Indian Sociology.
- M Jadhav, Dr. Ambedkar on Scheduled Tribes, round table India.
- DN Gautam, Education of Scheduled Tribe in India: Schemes and Programmes. , Vol.4 Journal of Education and Practice.

- Tribal society, Definition of tribal society, Meaning of tribal society, tribal problems in India, Indian tribes, Tribal way of life in India (2011), https://www.sociologyguide.com/tribal-society/index.php.
- Statistical Profile of Scheduled Tribes in India 2013 (Dec. , 2013), https://ruralindiaonline.org/en/library/resource/statistical-profile-of-scheduled-tribes-in-india-2013/#:~:text=FACTOIDS,50%20per%20cent%20or%20more.
- Schedule Tribes in India (Oct. 9, 2019), https://www.jagranjosh.com/general-knowledge/schedule-tribes-in-india-1448689214-
- Department of Social Justice and Empowerment Government of India http://socialjustice.nic.in/SchemeList/Send/25?mid=24541.
- SCHEMES FOR ECONOMIC DEVELOPMENT OF SCHEDULED TRIBES https://tribal.nic.in/downloads/NSTFDC/NSTFDCscheme.pdf.
- Upliftment of Particularly Vulnerable Tribal Groups https://pib.gov.in/PressReleaseIframePage.aspx?PRID=1705784
- Sumit Kumar Minz Tribal Development Policies in India: Its Implications and Prospects, mukt shabd journal, issn no. : 2347 -3150
- Shubhanshi Phogat. https://blog.ipleaders.in/role-effect-central-government-schemes-welfare-tribal-communities-india/
- Tribal Economy, https://egyankosh.ac.in/bitstream/123456789/69311/1/Unit-2.pdf
- GLOBALISATION AND ITS EFFECT ON TRIBAL DEVELOPMENT, https://www.ijirmf.com/wp-content/uploads/2016/11/201510032.pdf, Mrs. Sephali Pradhan
- Representation of Tribal communities in India, https://www.legalserviceindia.com/legal/article-5610-representation-of-tribal-communities-in-india.html
- Das, S. T. (1993). Tribal development and socio-cultural matrix (Vol. 160). Kanishka Publishers, Distributors.
- Ghurye, G. S. (1980). The scheduled tribes of India, Transaction Publishers, New Brunswick and London.
- Bhowmick, P.K. (1982). "Approaches to Tribal Welfare" in Tribal Development in India: Problems and Prospects, ed. By B. Chaudhuri, Inter-India Publications, New Delhi.
- Basu, Ranjan, Ashok and Nijhawan, Satish, Tribal development Administration in India Mittal Publications, New Delhi, 1994.
- Das , Kumar, Amal, and Roy Chowdhuary Kumar Bidyut and Raha , Kumar, Manis ,"Hand Book on Scheduled Castes and Scheduled Tribes of

West Bengal "cultural research institute, Kolkata 1966.
- Dr. Taradutt, Tribal Development in India, Gyan publishing house2015.
- Gardner, K. and Lewis, D. (1996). Anthropology, Development and the Post-Modern Challenge. London: Pluto Press.
- Lipton, M., and Toye, J. 1990. Does Aid Work in India? A Country Study of the Impact of Official Development Assistance. London: Routledge.
- Gandhi, M., & Sundar, K.H.(2019). Denotified Tribes of India: Discrimination, Development and Change, Routledge.
- Hooja, Meenakshi, Policies and Strategies for Tribal Development, Rawat Publications, New Delhi 2004.
- 13) Vyas, N.N. 1989. Tribal Development: Between Primordiality and Change in J.P.Singh and N.N.Vyas edited Tribal Development: Past Effort and New Challenges. Udaipur: Himanshu Publications.
- Registrar general & census commissioner, india ministry of home affairs 03 May 2013 retrieve from https://tribal.nic.in/Statistics.aspx, on 13.09.22
- https://tribal.nic.in/NGO.aspx on, 12.09.22
- https://timesofindia.indiatimes.com/blogs/voices/scheduled-tribes-who-are-they-how-to-mainstream-them/ on 9:01PM, 15.09.22
- 1) Indigenous Life and Culture --E Encyclopedia.
     2) Indigenous people --Mack Millan.